# FROM ROOTS TO WINGS: SUCCESSFUL PARENTING AFRICAN AMERICAN STYLE

## Beliefs and Practices
For
Academic Excellence & Cultural Excellence

by James C. Young, Ed.D.

Chicago, Illinois

First Edition, First Printing

Front cover illustration by Harold Carr

Copyright © 2006 by James C. Young, Ed.D.

All rights reserved.

Printed in the United States of America

ISBN #: 0-974900-04-4

# DEDICATION

This book is dedicated to my wife, Jackquline. She provided encouragement and support throughout my career and pushed me to finish the book. Further, she provided love and nurturing to our two children over the course of their development. I have always respected her dedication, judgment, knowledge, and understanding regarding children. She spent more than 30 years developing, nurturing, and teaching young African American children during the critical years of their schooling—kindergarten and first grade.

I also dedicate this book to my family—my son, James Clayton II, my daughter, Jamille Young Bradfield, her husband, William Thomas Bradfield, and their children, Kennedy Noel and Chase Alexander. A special acknowledgement goes to my mother-in-law, Mrs. Ethel Wallace as well as to my brothers, Paul, Richard, and to my sister Ida Dandridge. Without their constant cajoling, patience, and support, the book would have not been possible. Thank you, family!

# Contents

# ACKNOWLEDGMENTS

**Education is the passport to freedom.  Malcolm X**

This book was made possible by contributions from many families and friends I worked with over the past 30 years. They would always ask, "Where is your book?"

I am deeply indebted to my late parents, for without them I would not have been. Many thanks go to Dr. Asa Hilliard, the distinguished Callaway Professor of Urban Education at Georgia State University. He has been a mentor and friend during my entire career at the university. Dr. Russell W. Irvine, professor, Sociology of Education, Georgia State University (where I taught for more than 20 years), nudged me all the way to the finish line.

To those who implemented the family literacy program at Blalock Elementary School (located adjacent to the Bankhead Courts Public Housing Projects)—staff from the Center for the Study of Adult Literacy at Georgia State University, Toren Steele, Mary Hill, and Blalock principals Dr. Robert Lowe and Mr. Clarence Loften—I owe many thanks for what we learned from the parents and children we worked with for more than five years.

Much thanks goes to the staff of the Family Initiative Literacy project—Itihari Toure, Marcia Lynch, and the many graduate and undergraduate students from Clark Atlanta University.

I appreciate the support and encouragement I received from Linda Hassan Anderson, a stalwart for African American children and parents. She is a spirited leader of the Atlanta affiliate of the National Black Child Development Institute. Thanks to Penny Hicks, who directed the infant-toddler parent program at Carver Homes, where I spent more than a decade working with families, children, and youth.

From 1985 to 1989 I worked with Gayle Cunningham, executive director of the Jefferson County Committee for Economy Opportunity, to implement and evaluate the effectiveness of delivery services to parents in Head Start and the Parent and Child Center programs. Much appreciation and thanks go to her and her staff. Ms. Cunningham's insight into the development of children and program services provided the kind of sensitivity all university faculties should have access to in their day-to-day operations, for pre-service teachers seeking a degree in child development or early childhood education.

My colleagues at Clark Atlanta University also inspired me to finish *From Roots to Wings*. Dr. Leslie Fenwick, Associate Dean, School of Education, helped by providing continuous technical support to get the book completed. Dr. Melanie Carter, Chair of the Department of Educational Leadership, was unwavering throughout the process. She provided the kind of editorial assistance and guidance I needed to bring the document to completion. Thanks and appreciation is extended to Dr. Charlyn Harper Browne, Chair of the Department of Counseling, Exceptional Education, and Psychological Studies. Years ago she wrote an op ed piece for the local newspaper, in which she simply asked, "Do you want weeds or flowers?" This question guided her as she nurtured her son from birth to his enrollment at an Ivy League university.

Thanks to Dr. Bobbye Booker Coleman, a friend and former professor at Spelman College, and Roxanne Samuels Hose. The four of us, with Charlyn Harper Browne, were the original "Smurfettes" during their doctoral studies at Georgia State University. They called me "Papa Smurf."

I extend a thank you to Pearl Cleage and Zaron Burnett, novelists, from Just Us Theater. They raised the difficult questions about communicating the essence of my work when putting pen to paper.

A special thank you is extended to the students in my curriculum theories and parent education classes who assisted in the collection of data over the years. Their names are too numerous to list, but they know who they are. I want to thank each student who was enrolled in the 404 and 498 courses during the years 1991 to 2004. The collection of information from parents enabled each of you to have a reality-based experience with the root of our communities, African American mothers and fathers.

I appreciated the support, cooperation, and feedback from the many parents who always attended the workshops that I conducted at their respective schools or school districts within the metropolitan area of Atlanta and throughout the southeastern states. These parents gave me the impetus to, again, write the book. I also acknowledge the support I received from the many parents of my church— Christian Fellowship Baptist Church— who attended the 12 sessions of my Parent Education from a Christian Perspective workshop. Their feedback added to the countless parents who provided encouragement to produce *From Roots to Wings*. Sister Safiyyah Shahid, principal of the Mohammed schools, and the faculty were also very supportive and encouraging over the years I have worked with them.

I would be remiss if I did not acknowledge those faculty and friends from "Ole T.C.," now Winston-Salem State University. My freshman English professor, Carrie C. Robinson, made it possible for me to become a successful college student by teaching me how to write. The basketball icon, Coach Clarence "Big House" Gaines, gave me the opportunity to attend college. Leon Whitley introduced me to Coach Gaines via a telephone call. Leon, a former player for WSSU, had recommended a number of players from Philly. Thanks, Leon. A thanks also goes out to Gerald W. Johnson, my college roommate and lifelong friend. He served as a principal in the Montgomery County Maryland School District where he invited me to conduct numerous workshops for his staff and parents.

I want to acknowledge the support from the Conveners of the *Jegna Collective—Itihari Toure, our fearless leader, Judy Fears, Nkosi Diop, Dr. Asa Hilliard, Eniola Kalimara, Susan Mitchell, Dr. Will Coleman, Dr. Mark Lomax, Pastor of the First African Presbyterian Church, and Janelle Gabriel, a future contributor to the scholarship of our children. This group of scholars convenes a monthly forum where ideas and actions regarding the future of African American children, youth, and families are discussed and acted on. Chike Akua, a Jegna Initiate, and a prolific writer and educator, was always available for technical advice. Mrs. Elizabeth Cross, administrative assistant in the Department of Curriculum, provided the needed technical assistance to finish the manuscript.

*The Jegna Collective is a community. It is a group of people connected by the desire to strengthen our African spiritual power through African socialization. The word Jegna is taken from the Amharic language of Nubia. Jegna refers to those who are altruistically committed out of an unqualified duty to their people and nation, to teach our children the art and science of a politically conscious adulthood. Within the Jegna Collective there is an initiation process that have levels associated with the Dogon ways of knowing (Hilliard, 1997).

Finally, I want to thank Dr. Jawanza Kunjufu for his patience and support in making this manuscript a reality.

# INTRODUCTION

**"Unlock the genius in all children." – Dr. Asa Hilliard III**

*From Roots to Wings* was born out of my concern and passion for African American children. As an educator-scholar-activist, I have witnessed the increasing institutional indifference shown by public schools toward African American students, especially male students. This book seeks to reverse this demoralizing trend by sharing culturally grounded rearing and socialization processes that will prepare our children for academic and cultural success.

One of the many lessons to be drawn from my work in the community is that parents can learn from successful parents. I have learned from my own upbringing in South Philly, years as a classroom teacher, raising two children who are now adults, my Christian experience, my research with children, youth and families, and more than 30 years of university professorship.

I have been privileged to share what I have learned with many parents. Over the years, I have taught the following courses: Marriage and Family Life, Theories of Parent Education, Parent Involvement, Theories of Child Development, Strategies of Teaching, and many more. During my university tenure, much of my scholarly work—speeches, publications, research, paper presentations, and workshops—centered on socialization, self-concept and school achievement, child and preadolescent development, parenting, parent education, parent involvement, family literacy and education, and instructional theories for early childhood education.

I have served as a troubleshooter for many federally funded studies and programs throughout the United States and Caribbean that placed special emphasis on parent education and parent involvement. These programs included the Parent and Child Centers (PCCs), Parent and Child Development Centers (PCDCs), Head Start and Head Start Planned Variation, Follow Through, and Project Developmental Continuity (PDC). I have also served as a consultant to individual schools and to large and small school districts.

This book is influenced by the many parents, students, and scholars who remind us that we have the authority to socialize our own children (Hilliard 2004; Kunjufu 2003; Nobles 2003). We do not have to ask permission. We have been given a charge. Our ancestors are counting on us. Public schools are victimizing the masses of African American children, who are languishing behind in nearly every academic area through no fault of their own. Just take a walk through our neighborhoods and witness the result of a broken promise. When it comes to the education of African American children, I give public schools an F.

### Change Begins at Home

Attitudes and values that shape academic and cultural success are formed through the process of socialization. For children, this process begins in the home. It is in the home where parents have the power to mold the future. Through purposeful, skilled, and loving parenting, we can raise our children to become achievement oriented, highly motivated, grounded in culture and socially well adjusted for success in life.

*From Roots to Wings* is about successful parenting and socializing our children to be excellent learners. The findings shared will help African American parents embrace a vision of achievement for their children. I have found that the most successful parenting decisions and behaviors are informed by the following principles:

1. **Children are not clones of their parents.** Do not live vicariously through your children. Respect their individuality. I have a healthy relationship with each of my two children. We have wonderful times talking, throughout the peaks and valleys of their lives, because I use this principle to help me respect and appreciate the fact that they have their own thoughts and feelings about things. I will admit that this can make life challenging at times, but as my grandmother used to say, "This too shall pass."

2. **Your vision for your children can be achieved by taking action.** Most parents' dream of raising the ideal child. We fantasize that our child will be the next great scholar, artist, writer, composer, engineer, athlete, musician, architect, educator, or leader. How should we nurture our children to reach their full potential? Skilled and educated parenting is about taking action on a day-to-day basis to help our children realize those dreams.

3. **Good parenting is spiritually grounded.** From birth, children should be taught a system of spiritual beliefs that will enable them to draw on inner strengths and unseen resources. God is key to raising successful African American children. We cannot afford to disconnect from this Foundation of our existence. Spirituality is the centerpiece of African American culture that has kept us going in good times and bad.

Spirituality instills a strong sense of right and wrong from an early age. When we are guided by our moral compass, we become connected to the ancestors. This connection has benefits: it enables children to focus on academic and cultural excellence, and it empowers us all to rebuild the community/village.

4. **Do not accept what others say about our children and our people.** The media "reports" negative stories everyday about African Americans involved in crime, child neglect, and substance abuse—the list goes on. Far too often the movies and television shows that feature Black characters tell more of the same. What we seldom hear about are our stories of overcoming and achievement. If we are to raise self-confident children, we must tell them the truth about their history, culture, and unique selves. Only then will they be able to confront the lies about African American people with the truth.

5. **As parents, we must adopt the adage "each one, teach one."** If parents want to be successful, they must learn from those who have achieved success. That's what *From Roots to Wings* is all about. In chapter one, I'll present the findings of best parenting practices revealed by a survey I conducted over a 13-year period. The survey is a goldmine of information, and I encourage all parents to meditate over the findings and use them to enhance their experience of raising children in a hostile world.

In the movie **The Untouchables**, Eliot Ness (Kevin Costner) laments about the omnipresence of organized crime in Chicago. A police officer (Sean Connery) asks Ness what he is prepared to do. "If they shoot one of yours, will you shoot several of theirs? Are you prepared to meet them eye for eye? **What are you prepared to do?"**

To help African American children realize their natural genius, we must ask ourselves a similar question: What are we prepared to do to unlock the natural genius in our children? *From Roots to Wings* provides strategies that will help answer that question.

There are a plethora of books on parenting. The Internet can overwhelm you with listings of books and information on childrearing. Although they may provide good general information, our children are different, our culture is unique, our challenges are urgent, and we need more specific information on how to raise healthy, educated, happy African American children in a racist society. *From Roots to Wings* was created to help African American parents sort through often-conflicting parenting wisdoms and strategies that were never designed for our unique situation. This book will provide African American parents with a body of information they can use to make decisions regarding their children's academic and cultural excellence.

In this book we will also explore ways to reverse the demoralizing academic trends of African American students that are prevalent in far too many public schools by sharing culturally grounded rearing and socialization processes.

*From Roots to Wings* captures what I have learned in what might be described as an African American parent learning and socialization resource manual. African American families are often portrayed as being in a constant crisis. *From Roots to Wings* shows that such is not the case. This book identifies and extracts lessons from parents who have demonstrated success in socializing their children to achieve both academically and culturally.

The following poem was written by two lifelong, dedicated early childhood and child development educators who are also my personal and professional friends. They are a mother-daughter duo. The poem beautifully explains why African American parenting today is so important to the survival of our future.

**Our Children**

Who will sing our songs when we are gone?
When we are gone who will sing?
Who will keep our songs from vanishing?
    OUR CHILDREN
Who will lift each voice and sing out loud?
Who will hold their heads high and stand tall and proud?
    OUR CHILDREN
Who will learn from lessons that our songs ring true?
He watches over the sparrow, He is surely watching whom?
    OUR CHILDREN
Who will clap their hands and pat their feet
Who will nod their heads to our rhythms beat?
    OUR CHILDREN
Who will go to the mountaintop and tell it from there?
Who will spread our history everywhere?
    OUR CHILDREN
Who will preserve the chronicles that we have compiled?
Who will never have to feel like a Motherless Child?

OUR CHILDREN

Who will tread the same roads that we have trod?

Who will feel the bitterness of a chastening rod?

OUR CHILDREN

So

Who will overcome the trials of their day?

Who will triumph above obstacles in their pathway?

OUR CHILDREN

Who will trust in their own visions by remembering our past?

When we are gone who will make our songs last?

OUR CHILDREN

Burnece Brunson and Carol Brunson Day, 1999

# CHAPTER 1: THE FULL POTENTIAL MOVEMENT

**"The ruin of a nation begins in the home of its people." – Ghanaian Proverb**

**"We are all God's children." – Proverbs 22:6**

African American children are precocious, yet they are disproportionately underrepresented in gifted academic programs. To be placed in many gifted programs, a child must receive a teacher's recommendation and score 130 or higher on an IQ test—a test that has been deemed culturally biased by many educator-activists. Teacher recommendations are subject to personal preferences and prejudices, an unfavorable situation for Black children given that most teachers are White and female.

The Department of Education's Office of Civil Rights, National Research Council, found that Black and Latino students are half as likely as whites to be placed in gifted and talented classes (Donovan and Cross, 2002). In their article, "Forgotten pioneers in the study of gifted African Americans," K. Kearney and J. LeBlanc write:

"A significant body of pioneering research on gifted African-American children has existed for nearly 60 years and has been all but ignored in the field of education of the gifted. Whether by the accidents of history, the cultural milieu, or racism within the larger society itself, this literature was never significantly integrated into the larger psychological and educational literature about gifted children." (Kearney and LeBlanc, 1993)

The gifted programs nut has been a hard one to crack. It is one of the last bastions of White male privilege to stand against minority (and some female) inclusion. As early as 1924, one bold African American pioneer, Dr. Horace Bond, wrote the groundbreaking article, "Some Exceptional Negro Children" (1927), in which he passionately discussed the unfair practices in giving IQ tests to African American children. Dr. Bond stated that the "rules of the game" fixed the playing field so that White children always won in gifted placements and opportunities to excel while Black children consistently lagged behind (Kearney and LeBlanc, 1993).

Today our methods of testing and assessment have only minimally improved this dismal scenario for African American children. In the late 1980s, *The Atlanta Journal and Constitution* published an article that addressed the dearth of African American children's participation in gifted programs. The school district's explanation was that, generally, African American children did not earn at least 130 on the IQ test. The range of IQ scores for African American children fell between the low 120s to high 120s but below 130. At the time there were a number of factors that could have affected the performance of African American children when taking the IQ test. For example, the presentation of test directions from the testers who were primarily white could cause test anxiety. The use of language and or behavior that was unfamiliar to the children. Virtually all standardized tests rely on verbal language, both oral and written. The administering of test directions is very specific with little or no help from the administrator. Consider if children were asked to mark what he or she heard. A child (third grade) being testing for placement in classes for gifted is required to respond to unfamiliar language or to distinguish between pairs of words pin/pen, wreath/reef, and other foreign objects to identify. It was things like these examples that made the difference between being placed in the class for gifted or not. Efforts to elicit verbal responses through a set of procedures using rules not familiar to the children could easily have been factors that made the differences between passing and failing the test.

To remedy the situation, Atlanta Public Schools (APS) was awarded a grant from the Jacob K. Javits Gifted and Talented Students Education Program, United States Department of Education, which was written with the goal of increasing the number of African American students identified as gifted and/or talented.

The school district of Atlanta used the grant to implement a demonstration project to increase the numbers of African American children who came from economically challenging environments. These children were identified as gifted and/or talented, but whose needs for educational development were not met within the scope of regular school activities. Special efforts were directed toward recognizing and serving the needs of gifted and talented African American male children. Self contained, homogeneously grouped classes in grades 1 through 5. Teachers were trained to utilize multiple nontraditional identification practices that made it possible to recognize gifted and talented students, whose gifts had traditionally gone unnoticed. Behavioral and cognitive expressions of giftedness that are culturally distinct were codified. School staffs, families, and community members or agencies were educated in the use of the codified indicators in the nomination process. The overall goals of the demonstration project were:

- the development, implementation and refinement of an instructional program that met the cognitive and cultural needs of African American students in both content and process;
- the preparation of a cadre of teachers that were certified in gifted education, prepared in specific academic areas, and also trained in the cultural content and process needs of African American students;
- the establishment of a Family Institute that was designed to educate, encourage, and support family efforts to guide their children's development;
- the development of positive self-concepts among the participants in the project, with special emphasis on African American males;
- to increase the number of economically challenged students by 50% who were identified as gifted and talented in the demonstration sites; and
- to increase by 25% the number of African American males who were identified as gifted and talented in the demonstration sites.

Parents from high potential demonstration schools were invited to participate in a parent education workshop. I was invited to give the opening presentation. My topic was "Positive Parenting and the Elements of a Quality School."

The audience was made up of 457 individuals—434 were parents, more than 90 percent of which was African American. The other 23 were workshop leaders, teachers, administrators, and officials from the school district. It was from this presentation that I became involved in helping to increase the number of African American children placed in gifted and talented APS classrooms.

Parents needed to know what they could do to enrich their children's development. Over a three-year period, from 1990 to 1993, I conducted Full Potential Workshops for parents whose children were identified as gifted but could not make the passing IQ score of 130. The workshops were designed to:

- Help parents reverse the trend of low African American placement and retention in gifted programs by improving children's IQ test scores.
- Level the playing field for their children in APS gifted and talented programs.
- Identify best parenting practices and behaviors.

Thus, the goal of the workshops was to enhance both parent and student performance. I used the following characteristics of full potential parents, students, and schools developed by APS and the Javits grant as a guide in my work with parents. To help parents help their children improve their test taking skills, the workshops specifically focused on following administrative directions, use of time per item, unfamiliar concepts, and bubbling in on answer sheets as well

5

as on full potential student characteristics. I encourage readers to use these characteristics to set high expectations for your child, yourself, and your school.

**Full potential students are:**
- Confident
- Good thinkers
- Studious
- Expressive
- Good leaders and followers
- Self-directed
- Academically aggressive
- Creative and innovative
- Persistent
- Responsible
- Diverse in interests
- Willing to help others

**A full potential parent:**
- Meets children's basic needs of good health care.
- Builds up children's self-esteem.
- Lets children know that education is important to future success.
- Is educated in childrearing techniques and well able to confront the challenges of rearing children in today's society.
- Is knowledgeable about their child's school system and academic curriculum.
- Is involved in schools and PTAs. Is the teacher's partner.

- Serves as advisor, decision maker, and school and child advocate.
- Works with schools and lawmakers to set policies, develop curriculum, and ensure adequate funding for all necessary programs and services.
- Explains the ramifications of educational policies to apathetic or uninformed citizens.

**A full potential school:**
- Provides students with an awareness of their abilities.
- Enhances personal and academic growth.
- Provides academic enrichment.
- Instills a love of learning.
- Promotes student self-confidence
- Nurtures talent and leadership.
- Broadens student's perspectives.
- Increases student awareness of their connection to the global community.
- Assists student efforts to focus and find a sense of direction.
- Recognizes academic excellence.
- Recognizes artistic ability.
- Provides students with a vision of what they can become and believes that "all children can learn."

Prior to the series of workshops for parents, Atlanta Public Schools had three elementary schools with programs for the gifted that were located in the more affluent African

American communities. At the conclusion of the grant, that number had expanded to include schools in practically every area of the city. The number of schools had quadrupled. As of this publication every elementary school has a program for the gifted or the "challenged program" as they are now called. In a school where the numbers of potential students are small, those children are transported to a "challenged program" several days a week. As a result of the demonstration project, the school district established a parent education center, with appropriate staff and resources. The number of African American students, especially the male student increased significantly.

### *The Birth of the Survey*

The workshops taught me that although parents at times need guidance raising their children, they also have a wealth of knowledge about what works and what doesn't work. In 1992 I embarked on a journey that would consume my life for the next 13 years. I began to track and document the experiences and best practices of African American parents in the Full Potential Survey. Our motto was, "Aiming for anything less than excellence is unacceptable!"

Working with a research staff made up of my advanced college students, we followed African American families from 10 school-community districts in metropolitan Atlanta over a 13-year period. We selected families with K–6 children and K–5/6 (fifth or sixth-grade) schools. In all, we surveyed 5,000 parents, mostly mothers (80 percent of total respondents). We interviewed parents only once.

# The Full Potential Movement

Interviews took place at a variety of school-community meetings and events, including PTA meetings, parent involvement workshops, parent education classes, school-wide parent conferences, countywide parent gatherings, school carnivals, and statewide PTA conferences. Attendance at these meetings varied, from as few as 25 parents up to a countywide session with more than 1,500 parents. We also recruited parent participants from my Parent Education from a Christian Perspective workshop that I conducted at my church, Christian Fellowship Baptist Church located in College Park, Georgia.

All but two of our schools were public. One school was a private Christian school that met the grade (K–5/6) requirement. The other school was the Clara Mohamed Elementary School, a Muslim school.

At each interview, parents were given three 5x8 index cards on which they were asked to answer the following three questions:
1. What is an ideal child?
2. What are your beliefs about parenting?
3. What are your practices based upon your beliefs? What behaviors do you model for your children?

Toward the end of the program we asked a fourth question: "Do you celebrate Kwanzaa?" Approximately 30 percent of parents responded to this question.

Parents were told to write only one answer on each card in single-sentence responses or bullet form. At the conclusion of the interview, cards were collected. Parents were given time to talk about their written comments with one another. I will explore their insightful responses throughout the book.

## *College Student Survey*

The team also surveyed 331 undergraduate students from Clark Atlanta University, Morehouse College, Morris Brown College, and Spelman College using a tool developed by the High Scope Educational Foundation (Ypsilanti, Michigan). Respondents were enrolled in child development, educational psychology, curriculum methods, early childhood education, and parent education coursework.

The High Scope instrument was comprised of 53 student characteristics. Each student was asked to select 10 characteristics that best described the kind of student they would want in their classroom.

In the following chart, the APS/Javits list and college student answers are shown side-by-side to illustrate the similarities between the two groups.

| Full Potential Student (APS/Javits) | Ideal Student (College Students) |
|---|---|
| Confident | Self-confident |
| A good thinker | Desire to excel |
| Studious | Asks questions |
| Expressive | Determined |
| A good leader and follower | Cooperative |
| Self-directed | Creative |
| Academically aggressive | Persistent |
| Creative and innovative | Intelligent |
| Persistent | Socially well-adjusted |
| Responsible | Obedient |
| Diverse in interests | Healthy |
| Willingness to help others | Independent |

# The Full Potential Movement

(Other ideal characteristics given by college students were: friendly, competent in basic skills, versatile, affectionate, competitive, courteous, self-sufficient, receptive, is a visionary, energetic, thorough, is a risk taker, intuitive, courageous, sincere, careful, remembers well, critical, self-satisfied, industrious, talkative, emotional, and altruistic.)

Why are these lists important to parents? African Americans are often rightly suspicious of institutional frameworks and pedagogy. However, as you can see in the next chapter, the answers provided by the African American college students are similar or related to the characteristics developed by APS/Javits. These lists are important to African American parents because they provide a vision of what's possible. They inspire us to set high expectations for our children.

High expectations come with a price, however. Remember the question: what are you willing to do? As parents, that means we must take the necessary steps to help our children achieve those goals. That may mean some personal sacrifice: Reading a book with your child instead of watching television. Taking your child to church instead of sending him with someone else while you stay at home. Being consistent in disciplining children, even when you are tired. Getting to know your child's friends when all you really want to do is talk about adult matters to a friend. Loving your child even when she makes you angrier than you ever thought possible. Reworking the budget to pay for music lessons. Going to every game, assembly, and parent-teacher conference. Parents, your presence in your child's school can make an important difference in how he or she is treated academically.

# CHAPTER 2: THE IDEAL CHILD

"We are not raising our own children. We have no systematic socialization structures for the masses of our children. They are raising themselves or others are raising them. We have forfeited one of the most vital functions of a people, the responsibility for intergenerational cultural transmission." – Asa G. Hilliard III ("Twelve Challenges and Twelve Powers of African People").

If you noticed that the ideal student characteristics listed in the previous chapter are seldom connected to African American children in the media, you are correct. This is why we must teach our children to not believe what other people say about us. The truth is that our community produces full potential students year after year—and always has, even in the most impoverished, unhealthy, crime-infested conditions. When parents from various communities were asked to characterize what they thought an ideal child was, they collectively cited the following in no particular order: such a child was caring, loving, bright, honest, reliable, obedient, creative, patient, healthy, thoughtful, cheerful, helps out, and was respectful. When these characteristics are combined with the above list, and are used to mold and shape our children, we will come closer to having a system of socialization with a structure for the masses of African American children.

One of the important aspects of providing a rich foundation for young African American children is knowing about child development at the different stages. In the book, Awakening the Natural Genius of Black Children (Wilson,

1991), parents are reminded of the necessity of having knowledge of their children's development. Knowledge of child development enables parents to know what to do to stimulate children's intellectual development. The lack of knowledge retards the children's potential. For example without knowledge, our children are often denied opportunities to enrich their language skills and math skills. Parents must know that reading and speaking to children helps to develop good communication skills, regardless of age. Children mimic what they see and hear. Parents are children's first language models. Parents should read and talk with their children daily, if possible. Reading aloud is very important. This activity should occur throughout the years from zero through the elementary years. During these early years parents should provide lots of hands on activities. This lets young children opportunities to explore and discover on their own.

You want young children to develop language skills, use of their senses – touch, smell, sight, hearing and taste. You want young children to develop use of their bodies – large and small muscles. Things they do must be appropriate for their age and level of development. As young children's language skills expand you should encourage this avenue by asking questions, even if you do not always have answers.

As children approach the elementary school years, their bodies continue growing and developing. With proper eating and exercising, their bodies become longer, leaner, and more coordinated. The ability to use fine motor skills becomes more refined. Children become more self sufficient, responsible and independent. The school years (6-12) is a phase where children learn about the wider world and learn to master new responsibilities, attitudes, and behaviors that will carry them into adulthood. During this period, children are engaged in athletics and other physical challenges. They participate in games that are organized and have rules to follow. In addition their reasoning and thought processes continue to increase. Children expand their knowledge and understanding about self; they master different levels of literacy skills, and form friendships. Peer influence is a major part of this phase of their development. All phases of development continue to expand and are constantly being refined, i.e. physical, intellectual, social, and emotional.

The next phase of development is the connection between late childhood and adolescence. This phase will carry them into adulthood. During this phase of life the onset of puberty begins. Puberty leads them into adulthood and sexual maturity. Their thought processes becomes abstract and idealistic. They take more responsibility for their schoolwork and academic success. Their use their value-compass as a map to negotiate the larger world and establish independence from the family. These are some of the developmental challenges that all children go through. During these phases the most important factor for parents is to spend quality time with your children. In the long run the factor of quality time will carry more weight than things given to them through the phases they have just completed.

Now let's keep it real, as the children say. No child (or parent) is perfect. Each will have strengths and weaknesses. There will be good days and difficult days. On some days you'll look at your child and wonder where you went wrong. That's normal and natural. Remember, we are not our children. They come with their own developmentally appropriate agendas and personalities. When the gap between you seems too large to manage, refer to this book often. You will feel more equipped to handle the challenges.

We all love our children, but there are times when they truly try our patience. They test the boundaries that you've established in the home. But if they didn't test and try us we would wonder what was wrong with them. Rest assured, they're on their job, and as you begin to apply the best practices described throughout this book, you'll become more confident and skilled at handling whatever children throw your way.

Love, the bond that connects us to our children, gives us the patience to overcome most parenting difficulties. Ask any grandparent or great grandparent. They'll tell you that some of their best times were when they were raising their children. Parenting is both a joyful and challenging life journey.

If children were perfect, they wouldn't need us to help them mature. They are not perfect and they need us more than ever before. I present the ideal child for your consideration— not to frustrate you with an impossible dream, but to show you what traits you can develop in your own children to help them become more well-rounded, productive human beings.

The characteristics listed by APS/Javits and Full Potential survey respondents do not imply that our children are perfect. However, there are traits that children must develop if they are going to be successful in life. It's a given that they will have more of some and less of the other. As parents, we must build on their strengths while helping them to correct character flaws, low academic performance, social difficulties— whatever your child needs help with.

Take, for example, two sisters, Leah and René. Leah is a right brained, artistic type who has a vivid imagination. Her side of their bedroom is a mess, and her study skills are chaotic. René is a dominant left brained thinker, highly organized, and mathematic. Her side of the bedroom is always neat, and no one has to remind her to do her homework. Although Leah is artistic and loves music, she lacks the discipline to practice her piano lessons. René also loves music, and while she is not musically gifted, she loves to practice the piano. Through daily practice, René learns to play the piano competently. Leah is still at the beginner level in her piano studies even though she is musically gifted.

The parents of Leah and René can use the Full Potential characteristics to help their girls achieve balance. Leah needs more structure and René may need more activities that allow her to develop her creativity. Both girls are capable of achieving greatness, and it is up to their aware, skilled parents to assess their individual strengths and weaknesses and adapt their parenting to meet their needs.

Today we know even more about the power of setting expectations for our children. A goal achieved was first a dream. Let the Full Potential lists guide you as they have many African American parents over the years.

### *Full Potential Children*

The number one ideal student characteristic cited by APS/Javits and the African American college students was self-confidence. Without it, children do not perform to their full potential. Their gifts lay dormant because they're never quite sure about anything. Among African American children, bravado often masks fear and low self-esteem. If you've ever heard a young person declare that she has high self-esteem while at the same time wearing revealing clothes, engaging in unsupportive relationships, and failing in school, you know what I mean.

Critical thinking is an essential skill for your children to have in school and in the workplace. As they grow older, you won't be around to help them solve problems. Lay the groundwork early by allowing them to ask questions. Old style African American parenting says that children are to be seen and not heard. The essence of what the elders were demanding was respect, and that should continue to be instilled in our children. However, we must allow our children to speak up, in a respectful manner, when they have opinions and questions. Telling them to "shut up" or "be quiet" will not help them achieve critical thinking skills. Learning how to think and express oneself respectfully is essential to creativity (*kuumba*) and success in business, artistic endeavors, and life in general.

Regardless of where you stand on the leadership issue in our community, I'm sure we will all agree that we could do better. Let us start with our children. Self-confidence, critical thinking skills, and respectful expression naturally give birth to the ability to lead, as well as follow. To be a success in school and in life, children must learn to lead and cooperate with others.

I hear a lot of parents complain that their children are not as self-motivated as they were growing up. If that's the case with your children, let the list guide you in setting high expectations for them. Self-motivated (i.e., self-directed) students start and complete all assignments on time. They do not need constant prompting from parents to do their homework and chores. Self-motivated students are academically aggressive and persistent. They do not let anything or anyone get in the way of their education. Some parents may think this type of child is an alien from outer space, but you would be surprised. In my years of teaching, I found that some of my most self-motivated students were keeping this success trait a secret in order to be popular, just as Dr. Jawanza Kunjufu has stated in many of his books. You may have such a child. On the other hand, if your child seems too "laid back," perhaps he or she requires more structure at home—doing chores and homework at a certain, set time everyday, for example. Your child needs to learn that leaders are highly tenacious. They do not give up until the task is accomplished.

Children must also learn that there will be times when they will have to be good followers. This does not mean being mindless, but being responsible, obedient, disciplined, and able to follow through on tasks given.

The ideal child has diverse interests, which means that parents must expose their children to all kinds of healthy cultural activities, educational opportunities in the arts and sciences, and developmentally appropriate entertainments. This is how children grow up wanting to be a lawyer or a doctor or a fashion designer. How can they know what they want to do unless parents expose them to a wide range of experiences?

Lately, the media has reported that America is getting heavier, but the truly sad state of affairs is obesity among children. The African American community suffers from obesity more than any other group, and this has led to an entire host of diseases and ailments, many of them preventable. It's the parent's job to provide nutritious meals for their children and to make sure they receive plenty of physical exercise everyday.

Health also refers to mind and spirit. The home must be a safe and healthy place for children to grow up. Protect your children's minds and spirits from inappropriate music, movies, comic books, toys, television shows, and video games. The home must also be a safe haven from the streets. Do not allow those elements to cross the threshold of your home.

Finally, the ideal student is independent and willing to help others. As a Christian and African American man, I found it interesting that only a handful of our college respondents rated altruism as an ideal student characteristic. We must transform altruism into a cultural value through the socialization of our children. Our children must be taught, through example, that they are their brothers' and sisters' keepers. Ultimately our children will be responsible for one another, and the best way to learn is if there are siblings, cousins, play cousins, etc. in the home. Learning to share, give, and take turns are skills governments need to demonstrate. Let it begin with our children.

# CHAPTER 3: GIFTED AND TALENTED PARENTING

**"For nothing is impossible with God." – Luke 1:37**

"Nothing strengthens families more than when parents take an active part in the lives of their children, especially during the formative years of growth and development. These years lay the foundation for the quality of life. The home, school, and church must join forces for the sake of our next generation." – Asa Hilliard III

    African American children are naturally precocious and gifted. Although intelligence is not fixed at birth, our children begin life with a natural head start. The quality of children's overall experiences during infancy, early childhood, and the elementary years are substantially related to their measured intelligence, academic and cultural achievement, and pro-social behavior (Wilson, 1991).

    How do we sustain the natural head start our children are born with? How they are socialized is critical to their development and learning. Socialization is the process in which children develop their habits, values, goals, and knowledge that will enable them to function satisfactorily as adult members of society. Parents are the primary agents of this process. Children believe what you tell them and model for them, and they try their best to live up to your expectations of them.

    What is talented and gifted parenting? From the Full Potential Survey, we learned the following about effective parenting values, beliefs, and behaviors:

- Parents believed they could make a difference in their children's academic and personal development.
- Parents frequently told their children that they had high expectations of them.
- Parents had a vision of personal success for each child and a plan for making dreams come true.
- Parents told their children, in many ways, that personal effort was the key to academic success.
- Parents discouraged idleness and helped guide their children's time into wholesome activities.
- Parents demanded that their children spend 2–25 hours per week on homework, household chores, reading, family leisure activities, recreational sports, organized youth programs, and hobbies.
- Parents gave each child some form of household responsibility. This helped children to feel that what they did was important to the family.
- Parents set and enforced rules and regulations that governed the house.
- Parents had frequent contact with the school of attendance. They visited teachers, joined the PTA, and volunteered, when possible, in the class or school.
- Parents encouraged and inspired their children to strive for inner peace and love through spiritual growth and development.

Family optimism about the future plays an important role in determining school success. As a result of quality socialization experienced with parents or other significant adults (e.g., grandparents, close aunts, close uncles, cousins, and conscious care providers), children will enter school with a well-established self-concept. Self-concept influences the kind of school experience children will have. Research tells us the following:

- Attitudes toward learning are learned primarily in the home environment. Therefore, the home is central to development and learning. A love of or resistance to learning is shaped by the quality of exposure, enrichment, and enforcement of ideas, concepts, and skills that a child experiences early in life.

- The self-esteem of parents influences children's attitudes, academic performance, and cultural excellence.

- Optimal learning occurs when the home and school-community share in the educational experience. Parents must be proactive in their children's schooling. They must also be the primary force in educating their children. The educational needs of children far exceed what schools provide. In fact, inner city public schools consistently underestimate the capacity for genius in African American children. Educators like to say that their curricula meet state and federal guidelines for learning, but those guidelines have been developed on what is *minimally* expected from children. In affluent suburbs, the pace is faster and the expectations are higher. Coursework is often at least two grades ahead of inner city schools. And we wonder why our children are bored and not performing to capacity.

- Children learn best when their culture, which is learned in the home environment, is respected in the classroom.

- Parents gain in self-respect and feelings of compe-tence when they see themselves able to teach and influence their own children.
- Active parents enhance and enrich their children's ability, character, and development.
- It is important to share with school administrators and teachers the quality of socialization that has taken place in the home.

In chapter 1 we explored the characteristics of Full Potential parents developed by APS/Javits. Read the list carefully. How do you rate? Full Potential parenting can be summarized as aware, educated, committed, and action-oriented.

*Aware.* Excellent parents are constantly aware of their children, where they are, what they're doing—even when they are separated from them. Working parents have discovered numerous ways, such as cell phones, pagers, email, and neighbors, to stay in touch with their children. It is important to be aware of your children's friends—their parents, the music they listen to, the comic books they read, and the TV shows they watch.

*Educated.* Excellent parents continually refine their parenting skills. They study what works and what doesn't. Parental approaches are not cookie cutter one-size-fits-all because each child is different. What works with one may not work with another.

*Committed.* Excellent parents are committed to raising their children to the best of their ability. Earlier I mentioned the need to make sacrifices for the sake of the children. When you have a child your entire life changes, so get used to it. I have noticed that many who struggle with parenting resist the commitment. We all have feelings of love for our children, but that's not enough. Love and commitment go hand in hand. Love is a decision, moment by moment, and so is making and keeping a commitment. African American children are extremely needy because so many parents in our community have lacked the commitment to raise them. As a result, many of our children are raising themselves.

*Action-oriented.* Once they learn all they can about childrearing, excellent parents take action. They do what it takes to help their children achieve their goals. They help children draw out and develop their inner gifts and talents. Excellent parents go the extra mile in exposing children to positive cultural experiences that will develop their self-confidence, self-esteem, and knowledge about their people.

*Full Potential Parenting*

In addition to the main survey, we asked a sub-sample of 500 parents the following questions:
1. What is an ideal child?
2. What dreams do you have for your children?
3. What information do you need that will help you help your child(ren)?

Their insightful answers are summarized below:
1. What is an ideal child?  In addition to what has been said above, the following can also be applied:
   • Accepts constructive criticism

- An active and attentive learner, bright, critical thinker, questions, curious, enjoys school, thirsty for knowledge, inquisitive, intelligent, willingness to learn, yearn for knowledge, likes to ask questions, likes to read, loves learning
- Mature, responsible, dedicated, decision maker, sets high standards, motivated
- Clean and well behaved, respectful, neat and nice, well mannered, well dressed
- Confident, opinionated, expressive, high esteem, independent, interesting
- Constructive, positive attitude
- Caring, considerate of others, cooperates well with others, helpful, kindhearted
- Playful, cheerful, sociable, outgoing, energetic, jovial, liked by all
- Trustworthy, friendly, understanding, good listener
- Healthy
- Leader, zealous for excellence, visionary, task oriented, well rounded, willing to try things

2. What dreams do you have for your children?
- A career that brings happiness and provides for a family
- Long, prosperous, and productive life
- Become motivated to succeed
- Make good decisions
- Become whatever they desire
- Mature, respectful adults
- Blessed with God's spirit
- More opportunities than we had
- Break the cycle and finish high school

# Gifted and Talented Parenting

- Not become a teen mom
- Career oriented
- Opportunities to get out of being poor
- Complete college
- Positive influence on life
- Connect with and seek their dreams
- Productive citizen
- Develop a diverse portfolio
- Proud
- Entrepreneur
- Responsible
- Family after marriage
- Rich
- Financially independent
- Safe in a peaceful world
- Fun filled Christian life
- Solid education
- Go to college
- Successful
- Good morals
- Successful Black leader
- Grow up seeking God
- Take care of parents in old age
- Happy and healthy
- To get a college degree
- Independent
- To know the pros and cons of life
- Keep options open
- Travel the world
- Learn the best knowledge possible
- Well educated

- Live a respectable life
- Wisdom and a wonderful spirit

3. What information do you need that will help you help your child(ren)?
    - Additional knowledge and information about development and learning
    - How do you assess academic performance?
    - How to request activities from the teacher to help at home
    - Assistance with special needs children
    - Child development information
    - College information
    - Coping mechanisms
    - What study skills should children develop and how do they learn them?
    - How do you identify and find educational resources?
    - What questions do you ask during a parent-teacher conference?
    - How do you help children develop test-taking skills?
    - How do you start a parent support group?
    - How do you help prepare for standardized tests?
    - How do you save for college?
    - How do you help improve math/reading skills?
    - Are there programs to help young African American males?
    - How do you translate school statistics?
    - How do you know that the school curriculum is one that is excellent?
    - What books should we expose our children to besides schoolbooks?

- What constitutes a good after school program?
- How do we help children deal with boredom?
- Are there programs to help children achieve their dreams?
- How do we know if our child has a good teacher?

This is not an exhaustive list, but it does provide insight into many of the concerns parents have. The difference between successful children and those who are not has everything to do with decisions parents made while raising their children.

As African Americans, we know that our children are not born into a socially equal playing field. Perhaps that's why God made them so precocious at birth. He knew they would need every advantage just to keep pace, not to mention thriving at genius levels.

It is important for parents to know that a child's innate intelligence does not guarantee academic and life success. We learned in the gifted and talented workshops that as first teachers, parents have the ultimate responsibility of building on their children's inner genius, and we'll explore ways to enrich and stimulate a child's gifts later in the book. For now, just know that a child's intelligence grows or is stunted based on the types of experiences, exposures, enrichment, and other activities parents provide in the home. To build on a child's inner genius, excellent parents provide activities that are developmentally appropriate, meaningful, interesting, fun, and challenging.

*Beliefs Lay the Foundation*

Findings from the Full Potential Survey dramatically demonstrate that excellent parenting begins with a positive mindset and constructive life empowering beliefs. Not only must children develop self-esteem, parents too must believe in their own ability to care for their children. Without these traits, parents will not be as effective and today's wise-beyond-their-years children will see through their fear, confusion, and indecisiveness—and they will take advantage. Fathers and mothers in the workshops and survey were generous in sharing the following beliefs that lay a strong foundation for excellent parenting:

**Beliefs and Best Practices of Fathers**

- Act positive. Understand your children. Make sure they understand you. Have patience with them. Help them develop independence. Get involved with your children's homework. Get involved in the PTA or PTSA.
- Support your children in their growth and development. Encourage their exploration of new items. Show patience and tolerance for their behaviors. Assist them in developing their talents (inherent/acquired). Direct their behavior toward being respectful, polite, and treating others with respect.
- Teach children how to deal with both disappointment and success. Spend quality time with them.
- Show by example (try not to be hypocritical) and by being a good role model. Be involved throughout their education. Instill pride and joy. Have a good relationship with God. Enrich children's lives by visiting museums, taking sightseeing tours, exploring the outdoors and wildlife. Instill an appreciation for the environment.
- Manage children with a minimum amount of stress

and a maximum amount of love.

- Keep lines of communication open. Serve as a role model and support person. Show interest in children's education. Set educational goals at every level. Have an effective means of disciplining children. Praise children's positive and good attributes.
- Be willing to spend quality time with children. Show patience. Listen to them. Reward positive behavior. Give praise to children and others. Be present in their lives. Worship together. Teach strong moral and spiritual values. Visit the school frequently. Get to know all teachers. Show a willingness to discuss sensitive matters.
- Be attentive to a child's needs. These needs go beyond just the physical. How they feel (confidence and self-esteem) is dependent upon how you relate to them. Know that some days are better than others. Being able to talk on a mature level with them is important.
- Establish daily responsibilities for your children. Transmit those values that help to build a strong family. Show love and care throughout their development.
- Talk to other parents. All basically go through some of the same hoops when raising children.
- Teach children about their identity. Teach them to have self-respect and to respect others. Never neglect to give then spiritual guidance. Teach them about the Bible or the Koran.

## Beliefs and Best Practices of Mothers

- Steer your child in the right direction. Each child should be guided by his or her moral compass.
- Keep children away from drugs and out of harm's way.
- Encourage and give full support to children. Show

them love and give them values and morals.
- Provide your children with insights on life.
- Expose your children to music, art, and other literacy activities.
- Provide learning opportunities in their daily lives. Encourage them to develop their God-given talents. Challenge them to contribute to their well-being and the broader community.
- Help your children apply principles of right and wrong in their daily lives, i.e. home, school, church, and community.
- Think of the best for your children.
- Listen and communicate with your children *daily*.
- Attend church or the mosque with your children.
- Motivate your children with high expectations.
- Become knowledgeable and understanding about childhood development and their needs at every stage. Seek information to keep abreast and become a better parent.
- Give praise and get involved in the school and church with your children.
- Provide a wholesome environment where the children can grow and develop.
- Allow your children to express their feelings and concerns in a positive manner.
- Let them feel as though they are part of the family.
- Commit yourself to the full development of your children.
- Give children unconditional love.

We know little about the development of parental belief systems and their impact on parental behavior and children's development (Goodman 1992; McGuillicuddy-DeLisi 1992; Sigel

1992). For example, McGuillicuddy-DeLisi (1992) reported that mothers' beliefs about how children learn were related to measures of children's development but not to maternal behavior. Among fathers, beliefs were related to paternal behavior, but unrelated to children's cognitive development. McGuillicuddy-DeLisi argued that the failure to find a relationship between parental behavior and child development for mothers may indicate that a belief system may reflect a more pervasive orientation in childrearing which may not be observed in a particular episode or instance of parent-child interaction.

There is substantial evidence to suggest that belief systems, especially parents' sense of efficacy in relation to their children's development, may be related indirectly, if not directly, to child outcomes (Gray, 1993). In case studies of low-income African American families, parents of successful students viewed themselves as having a potent influence on their child's school and life success (Berreuta-Clement, 1984). Parents in these studies actively monitored their children's school progress. They met periodically with school personnel and actively constructed home environments supportive of educational achievement.

The researchers also found that parental efficacy in childrearing was a significant predictor of general parenting skill and of parents' support for their infants' intellectual development in three groups of low-income mothers. Parents who thought it was important to read and talk with young children were vigilant about health care and provided developmentally appropriate stimulation and play materials.

Simply, the more you believe in your own ability to develop full potential traits in your child, the more likely your child will begin to develop those traits. That is the power of the committed, informed, action-oriented, *loving* African American parent. ***From Roots to Wings!***

# FROM ROOTS TO WINGS:
## Successful Parenting African American Style

I am fascinated with the Baobab tree, which is why an illustration of one graces the cover of this book. The Baobab tree was named in honor of Michel Adanson, a naturalist who first saw one in Senegal, Africa, around 1750. A carbon analysis from one Baobab tree indicated that it was ancient, about *3,000 years old.*

The Baobab tree is different from other trees. It is a tree of great distinction and enormous proportions. For example, 15 adults can join outstretched arms to cover the circumference of a typical Baobab trunk. One ancient Baobab tree in Zimbabwe is so large that up to 40 people can find shelter inside its trunk. Other Baobabs have housed a small shop, a home, a storage barn, and even sheltered a bus.

The Baobab tree is the perfect symbol of African American parenting. Like the Baobab tree, we parents must provide food, shelter, water, and more for our children. The illustration on the cover of the book shows a family etched into the trunk of the tree. The mother embraces her child while the father embraces them both. The father-mother-child connection serves as a model for the African American family to regain and rekindle its strengths as outlined by Robert Hill in *Strengths of the Black Family* (1972). In Hill's book he outlines five assets of African American families – strong achievement orientation, strong work orientation, flexible family roles, strong kinship bonds, and strong religious orientation. A re-kindling of these charac-teristics would move us in the direction of restoring the "village." Within a safe haven of unconditional acceptance and love, a child will blossom (socialize) into a well-adjusted, productive adult.

There are at least three critical aspects of parenting that give shape to the adults our children will become.
1.  **Quality of interaction.** Do you spend quality time with

your children on a consistent basis, or are there periods of neglect? When you sit down to talk are there frequent interruptions (the telephone, television, the doorbell, etc.)? Treat your children the way you want to be treated. Give your child your undivided attention. Do not allow outside distractions to interfere with your interactions with your child.

2. **Parenting style.** There are basically three styles of African American parenting: permissive, strict (authoritarian), and enlightened. The least effective style is permissive. Children are allowed to run amuck, seemingly with no supervision. Children make decisions without limits or guidance. In the African American community, permissive parenting is often masked with harshness and inconsistent enforcement of discipline. If you've ever seen a child run around in a store after the parent has shouted, cursed the child out, and threatened the child with a beating, then you know what I'm talking about. The child learns to take the threats of a permissive parent with a grain of salt.

Then there are those parents, authoritarians, who do not make idle threats. As we say in the community, "They don't take no stuff." Parents using this style are unyielding and harsh. Children have no say in what happens to them. Parents are rigid disciplinarians and rule with an iron hand. As a result, children tend to be negative in their development and behavior.

Full Potential survey findings reveal that enlightened parents are the most effective. They do not feel that they are giving up parental power and control when they allow their children to participate in decisions that impact them. Enlightened parents permit some freedom in the choices children make. While these disciplinarians are firm and set limits, they are not like authoritarians. Enlightened parents take time to explain and reason with their children. Children raised in this style tend to be self-sufficient, responsible, and caring.

3.  Knowledge of developmental stages. It is important to know what to expect during each developmental stage of a child's life. Ignorance in this area has been the source of much parental confusion, and sadly, in extreme cases, abuse and neglect. Children who enter kindergarten without knowing their ABCs and 123s are suffering from parental ignorance. These parents apparently don't know that their children are reading and math geniuses waiting to happen—and that they are eager to learn! Poor language skills are the result of uninformed parenting. If a parent does not believe that little ones can communicate with adults until the age of two, the parent will have missed numerous opportunities to develop the language and communication skills of the child. When you know what to expect during each stage, your confidence as a parent grows, your relationship with the child improves, and your role as first teacher becomes more effective.

From 1994 to 2004, the Department of Curriculum at Clark Atlanta University (where I serve as a professor of Early Childhood Education) celebrated the theme "Awakening the Natural Genius in Black Children" during the Week of the Black Child. One year, our keynote speaker shared a personal story that she experienced during her pregnancy. A 37-year-old first time mother-to-be, she noticed while rocking on her porch a difference between her lawn and her neighbor's. Her neighbor's lawn was immaculate, with plenty of beautiful flowers ringing the perimeter of the grass. In stark contrast, her lawn had weeds.

The light suddenly went on! If you want flowers, you have

to nurture them. To begin with, the soil must be rich with proper plant nutrients. Watering must occur on a frequent basis, and the seeds must receive lots of sunshine. Flowerbeds must be weeded to provide a supportive environment.

Early socialization and education (watering, seeding, weeding) contribute to the development of academic and cultural excellence. The speaker reported that she once heard her son utter that he wanted to know everything. She knew at that point she wanted flowers and not weeds.

One of the most revered, respected, and much needed professionals in our community is the babysitter. Babysitters and working parents form powerful teams whose mission is to guide baby through the first years of life. In Africa, there is also a tradition of babysitting. It is called *kindezi*, and as parents, we can learn much from these caring individuals.

"Kindezi, the art of babysitting, is an old art among Africans, in general, and the Bantu, in particular. It is basically the art of touching, caring for, and protecting the child's life and the environment (kinzungidila), in which the child's multidimensional development takes place. The word 'Kindezi,' a Kikongo language term, stems itself from the root verb lela, which means to enjoy taking and giving special care." (Fu-Kiau, 1988) From this ancestral connection, Fu-Kiau tells us that in African civilization Kindezi is the greatest honor that can be bestowed upon an elder. Elders are considered as being spiritually strong and have a major responsibility of nurturing the young. This intergenerational connection provides for continuity, consistency of value formation and transmission of the culture. It appears to me that if we connect Hill's work and that of Fu-Kiau, the idea of the "village" to raise children would be again a reality.

As a parent you must decide early whether or not you want weeds or flowers. The growing and development of flowers takes tender loving care and continuous nurturing. "There is no more serious work for us than to do our part to regain primary control of socialization over our children, and to base our design for contemporary African American education in the best of our traditional structures. An African American education process is anchored in a nurturing process derived from an African view of the world, and a shared understanding of our environment and our existence in it." (Hilliard, *African Power,* 2002)

## Untitled

When you change your thinking
You change your beliefs.
When you change your beliefs
You change your expectations.
When you change your expectations
You change your attitude.
When you change your attitude
You change your behavior.
When you change your behavior
You change your performance.
When you change your performance
You Change Your Life!
Author Unknown

# CHAPTER 4: PARENTS AS TEACHERS

"Academic Excellence—NABSE recognizes the fact that education includes training, socialization, and enlightenment. Education is teaching someone what, how, when, and why to do something. Quality education in a democratic society requires that the educational process help all individuals and groups to be educated to do all of these things." – National Alliance of Black School Educators

"Cultural Excellence—NABSE recognizes that culture consists of the behavioral patterns, symbols, institutions, values, and other human-made components of society and is the unique achievement of a human group which distinguishes it from other groups." – National Alliance of Black School Educators. A broad panel of educators that would have to be considered blue ribbon formed these definitions. They represented the academy, the superintendency, the research community, and a broad base of advocates/activists.

At its annual convention in November 1983, the president of the National Alliance of Black School Educators (NABSE) appointed members to work on the Task Force on Black Academic and Cultural Excellence. The task force was co-chaired by Dr. Asa Hilliard and Dr. Barbara Sizemore. It had one year to present its findings and recommendations.

NABSE issued its report, "Saving the African American Child," in November 1984. It was an important document then and remains so today. It was a plan with a designed educational vision. The vision included the organization's perspective on academic and cultural excellence. Works by Dr. W.E.B. DuBois (*The Souls of Black Folk*) and Dr. Carter G. Woodson (*The Mis-education of the Negro*) strongly influenced the task force as they analyzed the conditions within which African American children are educated.

According to the above definitions of academic excellence and cultural excellence, it is clear that public education, as it operates in the African American community today, does not come close to NABSE's vision. According to the Joint Center for Political and Economic Studies (November 2000), African American illiteracy saw steady, indeed drastic, declines post slavery. In 1890, nearly all blacks were illiterate because of immoral laws that made it illegal for an African to learn how to read. Due to sheer desire and determination, in 1910, African American illiteracy was down to 33 percent. By 1979, illiteracy was down to 1.6 percent (Cantave, 2000).

Today, African American illiteracy is up to 44 percent! Two-thirds of African American students and almost half of all children in the inner cities are functionally illiterate, according to the National Assessment of Educational Progress (Hombo, 2000).

Reading truly is fundamental because it provides the foundation for learning in all other academic areas. On a recent segment of the TV news magazine *20/20,* American Idol winner Fantasia Barrino publicly revealed that she was illiterate. How did not being able to read affect the life of this talented African American woman? She said that reading even simple words was difficult for her. While competing on American Idol, she would fake the scripts, apologizing when she mispronounced words. She can't read contracts or record deals. Dangerously, she just signs where the lawyers tell her.

There is a legacy of illiteracy in her family, so no one noticed that she was struggling. Education was not a priority because she could sing, so she dropped out of school. Fantasia says that the thing that hurts the most is that she can't read to her four-year-old daughter, Zion. Fortunately for Fantasia and Zion, she's now learning how to read with the help of tutors.

Before Fantasia became rich and famous, she suffered all the slings and arrows of the illiterate life. And although she finally escaped the worst side effects of not being able to read, many have not been as fortunate. Illiteracy has contributed to high rates of unemployment and low income, imprisonment (nearly half of inmates read at the 6th grade level or below), and suffering of preventable diseases in our community.

If public schools have failed by not teaching our children this most basic of skills, then what else aren't our children learning?

Skilled parents are raising genius children all the time, often with little support from public schools. Parents must take their role as first teachers seriously. This is a life or death issue, and that is no overstatement.

In addition to core subjects, we must consider how culture is being transmitted to our children in school. What lessons are they learning there? Is multiculturalism really helping our children develop self-worth, or is this more false wisdom that has little to do with the unique needs of our community?

By infusing cultural excellence into the process of education, African American students, our children, would become problem-solving members of the community and the world. The responsibility of cultural development is up to parents and the African church. Schools play a role, but to a lesser degree because of other extenuating factors, including the presence of other ethnic groups, adversarial bodies, and limited inclusion by school district policies.

The mother is the first teacher of children. Messages received from her are carried into the world, thus beginning the child's world view. Teaching young children is a formidable task. To learn, young children must develop appropriate behaviors, which facilitate the mastery of knowledge, skills, and concepts. Teaching children is one of the more natural functions performed by parents.

"Parenting refers to the person(s) responsible for the nurturance and guidance of the child through its developmental periods into adulthood. The focus is on that person(s) or significant others in the life of the child who, by the nature of the relationship, fulfills primary parenting tasks. This person(s) who is defined as a parent by responsibilities, must recognize that parenting is a job requiring skills: If performed within the context of parental 'love' the process of child development is enhanced. However, if performed in an atmosphere of contempt and rejection, the process can be detrimental to development." (Willie and Reddick, 2003).

Children are not born with attitudes, a value system, knowledge, or a personality. They are born with a body, innocence, and in most instances, a healthy mind. The interactions between parents and children are essential because they lay the foundation for the developing self-concept. Parents who understand the importance of their interactions and behaviors with children focus on enriching the experiences and exposures provided. Conversely, parents who are ignorant of the developmental needs of children miss many opportunities to help their children learn and grow.

All children deserve parents who want them and love them. Children deserve a good home and a supportive environment. It takes two responsible, caring adults to raise a child from infancy to young adulthood. Parenting is an awesome job that requires an enormous amount of time, energy, attention, and resources. Children are not born with any attitudes or value system. These are learned through time. Their original self-image is formed in the family circle. Ideas of who they are will be developed in relation to the behavior of the people around them, particularly the adults (parents).

The emotional climate that exists in the home is the most important factor in determining whether or not children will develop self-confidence and self-acceptance. Long before children are able to reason things out, even before they are clear about the physical boundaries of their own bodies, they are aware and sensitive to the feelings that exist all around them.

Infants do not know where they end and the world begins. Particularly with their mothers and other significant adults, they first experience both self and world as one. Since they have no background of experience to compare to present situations, their perceptions of the way they are treated loom large in affecting their concepts of self-world. When children have confidence in themselves, learning becomes easier and stress is significantly reduced.

# FROM ROOTS TO WINGS:
## Successful Parenting African American Style

A major drive of the human body is to reach and maintain a state of balance. Periods of imbalance—hunger, pain, poor body position, and the like—are periods of discomfort, while periods of fullness, warmth, being held, and rocked are those of comfort. If crying infants, who spend most of their waking hours being comfortable, receive fairly immediate responses to their cries of discomfort, they begin to develop the idea that the world is a pretty good place and that they must be good people to be kept this comfortable. If on the other hand little is done to meet their needs, if long periods of discomfort persist despite all their efforts, then they develop the feeling that the world is not so hot, that they do not rate, and that they have little control over the environment.

The progression of time is important in the socialization process. Single emotional events are not as important as the general climate of love and support that exist in the home over the years. If, on the whole, day after day and month after month, children experience more comfort than discomfort, more balance than imbalance, more attention than lack of it, they will see themselves and the world as okay. They will develop a resiliency that will enable them to withstand the painful events that every soul suffers from time to time (and that we cannot always protect them from). So parents, no one's perfect. If you make mistakes now and then, don't panic. Consistently providing love, safety, and learning will make the positive impact.

As children develop language and reach out for more experiences, their need for acceptance, love, and warmth continue. As the cultural demands grow and the do's and don'ts increase, they need to feel assured of their place in the family.

# Parents as Teachers

By the third year of life, as they reach the stage of development where they are beginning to see themselves as separate and distinct from others, their need for support is critical. Children's behavior during this so-called "negative stage" (so-called "terrible two's and three's") can be viewed as an attempt to define themselves as apart from parents. While this can be wearing on parents, it is a necessary and vital step in the process of growing up. Acceptance is so important at this time because their willful behavior is harder to accept.

People no longer see your child as "cute"; pressure to conform to the old ways of parenting may increase. Now more than ever, children must have their parents' unconditional love and acceptance so that they can begin to see themselves as unique individuals with rights, privileges, and needs of their own. This is important in developing and maintaining their self-worth.

Now would be a good time to mention that a sense of humor is a must for parents of toddlers—in fact, children of any age. There will be times when you will wonder why you had children in the first place (please smile). Hopefully, those times are few and far between.

Studies of parent training and parent-child interaction in the home environment indicate that quite specific dimensions of parental behavior have substantial influence on young children's intellectual development. These potent parental behaviors include providing developmentally appropriate toys, structuring children's play, extending and facilitating children's problem-solving skills, and stimulating and responding to children's inquiries both emotionally and verbally.

Children develop mentally and physically by participating in running, throwing, catching, jumping, climbing, and leaping games. These activities develop large muscles and give children opportunities to gain self-confidence. By playing with legos, puzzles, and other games, children develop hand-eye coordination and pro-social skills as they play with others. These activities also foster the development of leadership and language skills and the ability to set and abide by rules and regulations. Children learn to take turns, wait on others, and make judgments. When children engage in activities that challenge their thinking, they are exercising the brain.

As children continue to grow and develop, crises will occur. These include the birth of younger brothers and sisters, the entrance into preschool or kindergarten, the intermediate years, and the beginning of puberty. In all of these, children build upon the original foundation of love, warmth, and acceptance laid down during infancy and the early childhood years. If this foundation is solid, chances are that self-confidence and self-esteem will withstand the sieges laid upon them by the pressures of life.

Parental acceptance is not synonymous with lack of order, limits, or standards. Indeed, accepting children at their own level implies that the parent recognizes certain limits. While children need to explore, this does not mean they can have the run of the streets. Safety limits need to be set—on their person, on other people, on objects that are valued by the family. Acceptance means setting limits that are appropriate to the child's level of growth and understanding and resetting limits as they grow so that they can exercise greater choices and greater self-control. Feelings of self-worth cannot grow unless experiences appropriate to a child's developmental stage are provided.

# Parents as Teachers

## *Make Learning Fun*

Little ones are hungry to learn. That's why they ask so many questions! Sometimes parents find it a challenge to come up with interesting projects to keep them occupied, but it is essential to the formation of your child's mental, physical, and affective abilities that you get them away from the television and harsh music and into more productive learning activities.

Parents have told me that they don't know how to teach their children. How do you teach a child to count or read? I tell them that every moment has teachable opportunities, and if you're committed to excellent, full potential parenting, you will come up with creative ways to teach your children.

Road trips provide numerable opportunities for learning. On particular trip, one mother, whose young daughter was afraid of the pre-rain lightening bolts electrifying the heavens, slyly devised a counting game to deflect her fear. Every time lightening struck, they counted. The child reinforced her counting skills while transforming her fear in the process. One time they counted more than 100 lightening bolts before they got home! Could this simple early learning counting game have led to this child scoring the highest math score on her seventh grade national Iowa exam in her school (nine out of nine percentile)?

Young children can count the number of blue cars or red cars (or any other color) they see on the highway. Siblings can make a game out of who counts the most cars.

Do you have a jar with change in your home? Very young children can count the coins while older children can learn to compute the values of pennies, nickels, dimes, and quarters. This activity is excellent for mental math computation and also teaches early lessons in saving and the value of money.

Counting and music go together because musical rhythms are based on numeric formulas. One father taught his daughter to count by singing and clapping number songs, which he would make up on the spot. Not only did they both have fun with this creative learning activity, it was an excellent opportunity for father and daughter to spend quality time together.

Reading is so important I cannot stress it enough. From the moment your baby is born (some say even while still in the womb), start reading aloud to your child. The secret to teaching a child to read is one that excellent parents have known for a long time. You can teach a child to read by reading aloud to him or her. That's it! Every night, before my children went to bed, either I or my wife would read to the children. They absolutely loved it and would sometimes want us to read one book over and over again, sometimes in the same evening! This may have been a ploy to delay going to sleep, but the point is, children love the stories. Reading a favorite story many times leads to memorization, which eventually leads to reading. Looking at the pictures, they may even make up their own stories. This is a natural part of learning to read, so don't criticize and tell them that they are not reading what's on the page.

In addition to reading to her child every night, one enterprising mother wrote words in red on large index cards and taped them to the items they represented (e.g., "chair" on a chair). Her daughter entered kindergarten reading at a first grade level.

Some educators may challenge me on this next suggestion, but for boys entering adolescence, developmentally appropriate comic books are a must to stimulate a love of reading. All too often, boys find reading tedious, possibly because school assigned reading materials do not interest them. However, all boys love comic books, and this enjoyable form of literature usually has high-level vocabulary words that will have your son frequently reaching for the dictionary. Warning: parents, monitor the content of comic books because many are not appropriate for children of any age.

One father, whose bright teenaged son had fallen behind in his grades, assigned him a list of African American cultural classics to read, including *The Autobiography of Malcolm X, The Isis Papers* by Dr. Frances Cress Welsing, *The Destruction of Black Civilization* by Chancellor Williams, and many others. In addition, he had to summarize what he read in a written report. The young man hated the assignment and hated his father, but he knew there would be consequences if he didn't do it. After a year of this challenging project, the young man had to admit that it changed his worldview and taught him many things. He said it was the hardest thing he ever had to do, but like any good and challenging rite of passage, it matured him. An interesting learning from this experiment was that when the young man had too much to do, he got much more quality work done in his classes. As a result, he brought up his grades and was awarded a full academic scholarship to a university in Wisconsin. Another learning was that no matter how old your children are, they will always need you, even when they are acting like they don't. So never give up.

As soon as your children are able to write, buy each his or her own diary. Have them write about their daily activities, feelings, thoughts, etc. This activity will develop and strengthen their writing skills while teaching them how to express their inner world.

I encourage parents of young children to keep the following items stocked in the home at all times: crayons, paper, yarn, buttons and other odds and ends, clay, glue, and safety scissors. These items are absolutely essential to children's creative and cognitive development. Let them draw and cut and paste to their heart's content. Some parents allocate space in the home as an art gallery to showcase their children's work. This is a great confidence and self-esteem builder.

An art teacher's art project was so fun and creative that parents must try this out at home. She had her students lie on the floor, underneath their desks, and tape a sheet of construction paper to the underside of the desk. They were to imagine that they had to paint the Sistine Chapel! Any educational activity that has children learning on their backs is a winner.

Another teacher in the primary grades had her children make fun African masks using construction paper, crayons, and whatever else was on hand. When they were finished, she taped their creations to the walls of her room. She says that not only did the children love the assignment, her classroom looked like an art gallery with museum quality work. Her students received many compliments from visitors, and of course their self-esteem shot through the roof. Parents, this is an easy, fun art project that you can do with your child at home. The self-esteem and cultural-esteem rewards are incalculable.

There have been numerous studies on the powerful effect of certain types of music on young children's learning abilities. I encourage all parents to turn down the rap when there are young children in the home and turn up gospel, jazz, and classical music.

These are only a few suggestions. I strongly recommend that you do what our Full Potential parents did: they shared experiences and best practices with one another in a *safe* way. I emphasize safe because all too often, parents feel that their families' imperfections are too shameful to be revealed; however, if you can overcome your reticence, you will soon discover that you are not alone. Other families are going through, or have gone through, what you're going through. Learn from one another. Your church should be a safe haven where you can share your frustrations and receive helpful suggestions. Talk to your pastor about creating a help ministry for parents.

### Socialization and the Influence of School

This section speaks to fundamental questions parents must address when they enroll their children in public schools, especially those located in urban environments. Parents must know who the teachers are and what role they play in socializing their children. As students, your children will develop a broader range of attitudes, knowledge, skills, and abilities to navigate in society. In some instances, the socialization from school can clash with the values of the home.

A child's first day in public school represents a new era in his or her life and a change in your role as well. Your children now come under the influence of new and different adults. These individuals provide supervision for a significant portion of the day. The school is now the agent for developing a range of behaviors, knowledge, concepts, and skills beyond the foundation laid by the home. In this transition, children become less dependent on parents and family and more independent as they learn to function in their new school roles. The socialization process continues but in a different context.

# FROM ROOTS TO WINGS:
## Successful Parenting African American Style

In accordance with the needs of society, schools usually socialize students to support and strengthen the democratic ideals on which the country was founded. Ideally, the school curriculum should be designed to fully develop all students intellectually, physically, affectively, and culturally. A purposeful school experience should be one that instills skills and values that will allow students to mature as contributing, productive adults.

Teachers serve as the bridge between home and school, and African American students will more than likely have their share of White teachers. Eighty-three percent of all elementary school teachers are white (Kunjufu, 2002).

It is the teacher who introduces young students to experiences and people who are generally outside of the family context. The teacher helps students learn new skills and attitudes that will help them to succeed in adult society. In this capacity, teachers become agents of the socialization process. A teacher's influence on the socialization process is second only to the family.

It is important that parents have a working relationship with their children's teachers. If the values, attitudes, and expectations taught at home are similar to those taught at school, the transition and relationship can be fairly smooth. Major differences, however, may seriously impact your children's ability to succeed in school. Although teachers are expected to accept each student's previous home experience, that is not always the case.

Teachers at all levels—elementary, middle, and high school—have an impact on the socialization of their students, but the earliest experiences in the educational environment have the most dramatic impact. From early school experiences students gain either a positive or negative perception of themselves as a learner and as a member of their peer group.

# Parents as Teachers

I have noticed that with their children's entrance into school, some parents feel their role has been diminished, but that is not so. Parents will continue to play an important role during all phases of their children's education. As a parent you must ask yourself, "What kind of involvement will best serve the needs of my children, the classroom, and the school?" Teachers must work with parents so that the needs of all groups can be met. However, in order to have the kind of relationship that promotes the interests and needs of children, the turf struggle must be addressed. Some of the problems between parents and schools emerge from differences in their view of who is in charge.

Now would be a good time to review the Javits/APS traits of good schools listed in chapter one. How does your school rate? What can you personally do to bring your school closer to this ideal?

When children enter school, it is vital that the school be a positive force in further developing children's self-concept. It is the school's responsibility to provide a variety of successful experiences for children. Scholars have reported that academic success or failure appears to be as deeply rooted in concepts of self as it is in measured mental ability. Successful scholastic performance creates feelings of mastery, which leads to high self-esteem. The reverse is also true. If your child can't read, compute, or keep up with classmates, he or she will feel low self-esteem. As a parent, it is your job to do everything in your power to help.

Clearly, continuous positive interactions between home and school are essential and can offset many potentially negative external influences on developing children.

# FROM ROOTS TO WINGS:
## Successful Parenting African American Style

Parents, it is true than when your child enters school your role changes, but that doesn't mean you are no longer teacher. In many ways, your revised role as teacher has just begun.

# CHAPTER 5: THE ROLE OF FATHERS

**"Even a child is known by his deeds, whether his work is pure, and whether it is right." – Proverbs 20:11**

**"As iron sharpens iron, so one man sharpens another." – Proverbs 27:17**

When Jackie gave birth to our first born, Jim, I could not have been more excited about having a son. My first thought was, "Wow! I'm a father!" Even now I have that same excitement every time I see Jim (or "Jam" as we call him)—even when I'm upset with him. Mothers often rule in the home when it comes to caring for children, but fathers must support them by stepping up to the plate with the children, especially boys. Girls and boys must both be raised to assume greater and greater responsibility as they get older, but they are raised differently.

Approximately four years after Jim we were blessed with our daughter Jamille. I felt the same excitement all over again, but the celebration was short-lived. Conditions surrounding Jamille's birth were different from that of our first-born. We attempted to replicate the same activities prior to Jim's birth. Jamille was not having any of that. She was practically born in the front of a 1969 Volkswagon Beetle. While sitting at home, Jackquline's water broke and we had to rush her to the hospital, which was located in Northampton, Massachusetts. The hospital was approximately 10 miles from Amherst, along countryside, one-lane roads. We called the attending physician, and he met us at the emergency entrance with all the appropriate equipment and staff. As soon as the near traumatic conditions were dealt with and Jackquline was comfortable, I went back to the thought of having a wonderful daughter.

## *Gender Differences in Child Development*

It takes more than testosterone to be a good role model and father.

Childrearing is not easy. Parents are responsible for the physical, emotional, and mental well-being and development of their children—a tremendous responsibility. Until the past two decades, for the most part, discussions on parenting had given little attention to fathers unless the focus was on their absence or dysfunctional behavior.

During the 1950s, 1960s, and 1970s, there was a proliferation of studies that examined the interaction between mothers and children, the influence of maternal behavior on cognitive development, mothers as teachers, mothers and children in the home environment, and influences of socioeconomic status on maternal teaching and nurturing styles. The importance of such studies is generally accepted, based on several assumptions regarding human development.

First, psychoanalytic theory emphasizes the importance of the early years on children's lives, the significance of children's relationships, particularly with their mothers, during the formative years, and how early experiences affect later personality development.

# The Role of Fathers

Second, an investigation of historical trends in child research revealed an early interest in such variables as intelligence and physical growth. Positive growth and development in these areas have often been attributed in great measure to the quality of interaction between parent and child.

Third, the mental hygiene movement focused its attention on prevention of mental illness; this led to an interest in identifying causal antecedents in childhood that lead to adult personality maladjustments.

Some research suggests that the differences in children's development can be attributed to the amount and quality of direct physical care the mother provides. Other researchers have attempted to examine aspects of parenting that are less overt. Feelings and attitudes were measured to determine whether or not they affect the parent-child relationship. Data from several studies revealed that maternal rejection significantly affects children's development. Other research and demonstration programs designed to assist parents in developing new knowledge of childrearing skills and methods of communicating with their children usually focused on the mother. The term "parent" was frequently used as though it was synonymous with the term "mother."

The omission of fathers from research was probably due to the fact that mothers were often the persons charged with the principal care giving responsibilities. The omission was also attributed to the following *erroneous* but commonly accepted assumptions:

- Fathers are unimportant in the childrearing process, especially during children's early years.

- Mothers accurately report what fathers think and feel.
- While mothers have a natural instinct for childrearing, fathers do not.
- Infants form strong psychological and physiological attachments to their mothers but not to their fathers.
- If one parent must raise a child, it should be the mother.
- Fathers only serve two basic functions in the family: they provide financial support and serve as role models for their sons.
- Human activities are deemed as either "men's work" or "women's work." In the late 1960s, new evidence began to unfold that challenged those assumptions.

New and different views began to emerge. Andrew Billingsley (1968), the African American sociologist who wrote extensively about race, described fathers' function as being instrumental—serving to maintain the basic physical and social integrity of the family unit, i.e., making provisions for food, clothing, shelter, and health care. Some researchers suspected that while it was the mother's job to respond to the expressive needs that maintain and enhance the socio-emotional relationships and feelings among family members, the role of the father is to provide novelty of stimulation that augments the routines of mothers.

Historically, the family in the United States had been patriarchal; the father has been the main source of authority and the principal provider and protector. That patriarchal structure supported the tradition of a strong father to whom children were submissive and obedient. Since "father knows best," he alone prescribed the activities, which were in the best interest of each child. His interest in the child was limited to the child's accepting and attaining goals established exclusively by the father.

In addition to determining goals for their children, fathers are shown to exert a primary influence on the development of their children's sexual behavior. Patterns of sexual behavior are greatly influenced by the differential treatment of boys and of girls by their fathers. Male children are more likely to be physically punished, whereas female children were verbally admonished for misbehavior. Fathers roughhouse with boys and treat girls in a light-handed manner.

The way children are treated strongly influences sexual behavior throughout the developmental process, even as early as the latter part of the first year of life. For example, a boy's perception of himself as a male, and thus as more similar to his father than to his mother, is an impetus for the boy to imitate his father. The work of some psychologists stressed the significance of the child's perceived similarity to the parent of the same sex, both as a motive to imitate and as reinforcement— the more the child imitates that parent, the more the child's self perception was similar to that parent.

### *Changing Times, Changing Parental Roles*

The status of women has gone through a steady revolution over the past 40 years. Changed social values have enabled women to select parenting as simply one of many career alternatives. Also, economic pressures have forced millions of women to work fulltime outside the home, regardless of whether or not there are young children in the family. As extended families became fewer, more families used childcare to help care for and educate their children. But professional childcare is expensive and not always available when needed. In many families, both mother and father are now sharing childcare and housekeeping tasks, just as they shared in the financial support of the family.   Although we are living in changes times, the role of mothers, historically and presently, has been used as the primary source for predicting children's academic achievement. Research conducted in education is increasingly beginning to examine the impact of fathers during children's early development and learning.

The level of father's education is a factor in what they do or not do with their children.

### *The Importance of Fathers*

An important factor in the development of a masculine orientation is the availability of an involved father or another significant older male. Boys develop positive masculine self-concepts when he receives consistent nurturing and positive feedback from the father (or father figure). Consistent access to father's time and attention is important for positive growth in this area.

Girls need daddy as much as boys do. Fathers help their daughters differentiate masculine and feminine roles, including appropriate gender behaviors and concepts of femininity. Studies have found that a significant relationship exists between girls' femininity and their fathers' expectations of their participation in feminine activities. One study concluded that daughters who perceived themselves as feminine were likely to view their fathers as demonstrating strong masculine characteristics of paternal behavior.

Even with the advent of feminism, fathers continue to view their daughters as more delicate and sensitive than their sons. Fathers tend to use physical punishment more frequently with their sons than daughters. They also tend to define all household tasks based upon sex-role appropriateness. Young and Hamilton (1978) argued that fathers actively encourage and reinforce children's sex typing, often through assignments of household chores. Fathers prefer that their sons perform outdoor jobs, such as emptying the garbage and raking leaves, while their daughters cook, clean, make beds, and, especially in African American families, help care for younger siblings. Whether such differential treatment by fathers is optimal in childrearing is questionable, but there is no doubt that fathers do have a significant impact on children's personality and development.

Interaction with a competent and involved father provides both daughters and sons with basic experiences, which they tend to generalize to other relationships with peers, male and female. We can safely assume from this research that children who have positive relationships with their fathers are more likely to obtain satisfaction in their personal and professional adult relationships with both men and women.

Clearly, the father is important to children's development and growth; yet early studies failed to give fathers the attention they deserved. Early college level child development, childcare, early childhood education, and psychology textbooks gave fathers practically no attention compared to mothers. Look in the indices of old parenting books and you will find that "father," "fathering," or "paternal" were either lacking entirely or limited to topics such as control of family (disciplinarian), aggression, absence of sex typing, or occupation and intellectual development.

A review of more than a half a century of research revealed that until the writing of Comer and Poussaint (1975), the African American father seemed unworthy of consideration, except for topics that put us in a negative light. Today, the ever-popular "how-to-parent" books also omit African American fathers. The focus has always been on White middle-class parents, particularly White mothers. Fathers have long been the forgotten parent.

What was revealing in my review of the literature was the fact that fathers were described as having very limited contact with their children, especially during the children's first few years. Fathers' roles were narrowly defined; their importance in providing a healthy environment for child development was often minimized, except in one or two isolated functions concerning sex-role orientation.

### *Redefining African American Fatherhood*

This limited perspective of fatherhood begs for a more active role for fathers in their children's lives. A more enlightened approach to fatherhood will have a positive and powerful impact on the developmental processes of children.

# The Role of Fathers

While in many families the father has assumed a more active role because of the mother's work schedule and career goals, it is my contention that there are more profound reasons for increasing and broadening the role of fathers. The late great world-renowned anthropologist Margaret Mead convincingly argued that children benefit from having two adults in their immediate family environment. When children are exposed to more than one adult role model, they learn that all adults are not the same and that living in a complex world requires the capacity to deal with different types of human beings. Mead also asserted that children who were raised in a two-adult household benefited from hearing adult conversations on a regular basis. Adult conversation is important in developing verbal and cognitive skills beyond the baby talk level.

Another argument in favor of redefining the father's role focuses on deeper issues of manhood, masculinity, and the authentic humanity of men. Fathers traditionally have been limited by their roles as protector, provider, disciplinarian, and transmitter of masculine values to their sons. This limitation cheated fathers from being fully human within the family context; they have been constricted by a narrow spectrum of socially defined behaviors, emotions, and values.

Many men are beginning to realize the negative implications of this often self-imposed, socially reinforced stereotype of being the family "money machine" who cannot display softer, caring emotions, who doesn't understand babies other than how to create them. As women became more independent financially and took on more of the tasks required to sustain the family, men found themselves in the precarious position of being unnecessary for their family's survival. Although this is an uncomfortable position for men, it is forcing many of us to face up to the fact that we must change—for the sakes of our families and ourselves.

- It is important to clear up some basic myths about African American fathers.

- Myth #1: African American men do not have a natural inclination toward parenting or nurturing. Reality: Parenting skills, like most other skills, are basically learned behaviors, not biological endowments. Social customs have taught women and girls to care for the young; social customs could also teach, encourage, and reward men and boys for the same types of skills and behaviors.

- Myth #2: Infants (male and female) show no interest in their fathers. Reality: When the father takes an active role during the early months of an infant's life, a strong bond is developed between them, just like the bond between infant and mother. Infants appear to be more concerned with the basic needs of nourishment, comfort, sleep, and a predictable, positive environment than with the sex of the person who meets those needs.

- Myth #3: There is a single and universal description of a "successful father." He is financially secure, emotionally tough, and has a natural strength and inclination to control his environment through rational thought and behavior. Reality: As women and men honestly raise questions about traditional sex-role definitions and expectations, both are acknowledging much broader characteristics and options for being successful women or successful men. There is no single definition for masculinity or femininity; neither is there a single or universal definition for a good father or a good mother.

- Myth #4: African American fathers do not want to be bothered with the daily routines of childrearing. Reality: Although traditionally many fathers have felt that their time should be spent on non-child related tasks, many fathers are eager to actively participate in direct interactions with their children at all levels. Many more African American fathers would feel this way if they were encouraged to realize their capabilities as parents.

Fathers were systematically kept from participating in the labor and delivery process and in post-partum interactions with mother and newborn. This exclusion and separation had an impact on the father's relationship with his child. After years of cross-cultural research, Santrock (2001) discovered several important principles relative to the process of father-child bonding.

- The initial hours of birth are particularly sensitive period as it is important for mother and father to have close contact with their newborn. Close physical contact between parents and infant immediately after birth is necessary if the infant's later development is to be full and complete.

- There appeared to be responses that were characteristic of mothers and fathers when they were first given their newborn infant. Fathers who watch the birth of an infant became strongly attached to the baby. (Santrock, 2001)

Fathers who interact with their infant immediately after birth form closer emotional ties than do fathers who do not have this opportunity. The period following birth is critical. It allows for a mutual responsiveness between parents and child that can have enduring effects on their relationship.

Many fathers who were not present at the birth of their offspring do develop a warm, loving, meaningful relationship with their children, despite the fact that the special moment was denied them or did not occur for other reasons. The challenge of childrearing is made somewhat less difficult when fathers and mothers share in the process of attachment during birth.

During the late 1970s and early 1980s, the American Medical Association (AMA) recognized the benefit of including fathers during pregnancy, labor, and birth. The AMA recommended that hospitals review their labor and delivery practices to include fathers every step of the way. It further encouraged fathers and mothers to share in the initial holding and eye-to-eye contact of the new arrival.

Fathers in general, African American fathers in particular, need to be more directly involved in the lives of their children. If not fathers, certainly a significant male role model is much needed during the formative years of growth and development. To get more fathers involved, we must do some things differently. We must redefine the role of fathers for present and future families. Let's examine some concrete strategies for accomplishing this change.

We must first remember that social behaviors do not change easily or rapidly; most people do what they do out of habit, not because of rational considerations. Parents raise their children, by and large, the same way their parents raised them. However, changes in our society will challenge us to break old habits and find new and positive ways of coping with modern childrearing. As we parents grow and change, we must remember that we are standing on the shoulders of our past, the ancestors.

## *A Few Ground Rules*

I present for your consideration some basic ground rules that will help both parents adjust to the changing roles of fathers in the family.

1. Fathers must choose whether they will assume an active or passive role with their children. The decision cannot be made lightly; being an active father will take a great deal of time, energy, and emotional stamina.

2. Mothers must cooperate by sharing childrearing duties and helping fathers develop new skills and understanding of the children. Mothers must be willing to offer moral support as fathers adjust to their new, more involved role, and there may be few social supports available.

3. Both parents must agree to cooperate rather than compete for the attention and affection of their children. The discipline,

the fun, the dirty diapers, and the hugs must be shared on an equal basis.

Fathers, your interaction with your child should begin at birth. Become a familiar, non-threatening person in your infant's everyday environment. How? By changing diapers, feeding, playing, bathing, and talking to the infant. During the toddler and preschool years, fathers can play a vital role in children's discovery of concepts, language, emotions, self-identity, and sexuality—the whole learning process of what the world is all about. This can be done by sharing activities and conversations, being sensitive to children's developmental stages, and demonstrating positive emotions and affection to children. When children enter school and begin to focus more on peer relationships, fathers can help bridge the gap between the family and outside world by attending teacher conferences, making random visits to the classroom, coaching sports teams, attending assemblies, talking about school at home, and accepting children's peer friendships. These activities should be carried out by dads during the various stages of child development.

So far I have presented activities most easily accomplished when father, mother, and children all live under one roof as a loving unit. The reality is that more and more families live apart. What is a positive, active role for fathers in situations of divorce or long-term separation? What about women who choose to have a child outside of marriage or adopt a child? At the risk of sounding simplistic, the role of the father (or significant male) should be as similar as possible to that of fathers in intact families.

# The Role of Fathers

What about single fathers? The number of cases where the father has primary custody of the children after a divorce is small but growing. Obviously, he will play an active childrearing role. However, in most cases, the father does not live with his children and is severely (and often unfairly) limited in the amount and type of contact he can maintain with the children. Such limited contact has no reasonable basis. Fathers should be encouraged to maintain as much contact as possible with their children. Parents should never allow marital problems to come in between the rights and responsibilities of parenthood.

None of the fathering activities outlined here is revolutionary. Numerous questions remain unanswered. What is certain is that families in America and particularly in the African American community are experiencing changes that will require new definitions, new styles of parenting, new role responsibilities, and privileges for both men and women. I am not suggesting that differences between men and women will disappear or that fathers and mothers will play exactly the same roles in all families. Mothers and fathers can and should determine how best to divide up the tasks necessary for raising healthy African American children and achieving a comfortable family environment. This division of tasks should not be based on stereotypes or myths about what a man or woman is but on emotional and social human values and the realities of day-to-day family life.

It is my belief, after having been raised by one parent and having limited knowledge of my role as a father when my son was born, that this redefinition will enable fathers, mothers, and especially children to have a world of richer experiences and higher expectations than ever before.

"Fathers, do not exasperate your children; Instead, bring them up in the training and instruction of the Lord" (Ephesians 6:4).

# Chapter 6: Ancestral Connections to Excellence

**"A stream cannot rise above its source." – African proverb**

African tradition holds that the birth of an African child is like the rising of a living sun. The spiritual nature of education must begin with a discussion about the innate cosmic nature of the child. From the mere thought of conception, the Spirit Incarnate, through a process of psychic memory, absorbs the thoughts, feelings, and experiences of the living ancestors from time immortal. The birth of every African child represents a link in the biogenetic chain of ancestral continuity.

The African child, this Cosmic Being, inherits the totality of physical and psychic power and potentiality from the ancestral/cultural soul, which must be nurtured and guided as an elevating key to our human growth.

Understanding the sacred relationship between the microcosmic and macrocosmic, the *Jegna* or midwife helps to shape this biogenetic cosmic being. Just as the process of true education pulls out that which is within (vs. training, which is forced *into* children by public schools), the *Jegna* also pulls out that which is within. From this point of view, education is sacred because we are sacred, multidimensional human beings. Therefore, any being that is pulled out from within should be done so with great respect and care because we are sacred beings.

# FROM ROOTS TO WINGS:
Successful Parenting African American Style

More than a decade ago, the renowned academician, Nana Baffour Amankwatia, a.k.a. Dr. Asa Hilliard, wrote *The Maroon Within Us*. This selection of essays about African American community and socialization contained a chapter entitled "The Maroon Within Us: The Lessons of Africa for the Parenting and Education of African American Children." Dr. Hilliard's insights provide an excellent guide for African American parenting.

Dr. Hilliard describes how missionaries, in their best efforts to "help" Africans, only wanted to impose their ideology on them—despite the fact that African history predates Christ. Every activity was designed to persuade the African to define himself in ways that best served the interests of the missionaries. Historically, African people have had a comprehensive and coherent spiritual point of view for millennia. The living ancestors are connected to their living descendents, and that's the way it has always been. However, with the missionaries' propaganda, Africans' heads became filled with ideas that were the antithesis of their traditional values and beliefs. This shackling of the mind made African exploitation easy.

African American parents must resolve two points of view in their childrearing practices: the Western approach, which focuses on control, discipline, and conflict resolution, and the African parenting style, which embraces the spirituality and history of the ancestors and the cultural environment of everyday life. Given that the African approach clearly defines the spirit of the child, the role of the ancestors, and cultural activities for parents to embrace, why have African American parents so willingly given up on what worked for us? A summary of Hilliard's work tells us that we tend to:

# Ancestral Connections to Excellence

1. "Equate sophisticated technology with culture, believing that such technology is exclusively European and that to affirm African culture is to reject technology.
2. Equate modern with technology, and to value modern as if it were cultural 'progress.'
3. Equate European culture with wealth and African/African American culture with poverty.
4. Associate education with the acquisition of all cultural forms of Europeans, and find it hard to conceive of educated persons who live the African/African American culture.
5. Equate self-affirmation with the hatred of others.
6. Equate religion with particular forms of European interpretations of Christianity and have not seen our own people as religious.
7. Accept the culture of others and have failed to study ourselves and to know our culture." (Hilliard, *Maroon,* 1995)

We must understand ourselves and how to parent our children. We have embraced the culture of others at the expense of our own history and culture. As a result, we have neglected and surrendered a rich African historical-cultural foundation.

Future generations must understand oppression from a historical context and how it continues to affect them. Since public schools do not care about teaching the truth to our children, it is up to us. If African American children are to develop the kind of confidence and self-esteem that lead to academic and cultural excellence, full potential parents must:

1. "Study and know their history and culture.
2. Model the behavior that is expected of their children.
3. Expose their children to the widest variety of experiences

imaginable, and do it continuously.

4. Recognize that parenting is a group endeavor and must engage relatives and friends.
5. Involve children in the real world of work and play, joy, and pain and truth.
6. Participate in organized groups that serve the interests of the larger group.
7. Give children responsibilities and hold them responsible.
8. Listen well to what children think and feel.
9. Tell and retell the story of one's people to the children so that they may experience continuity and know how to be." (Hilliard, *Maroon, 1995*)

Our community suffers from an acute case of cultural disconnection. Cultural disconnection occurs when critical information, values, and attitudes are not passed on to succeeding generations. When this occurs, entire generations suffer from amnesia. They forget who they are, and they are unable to become their authentic, genuine selves. We are witnessing this phenomenon today, not only in young people but adults as well. Let this book be a beacon for full potential African American parents. Everyday, instill in your children African-centered values that will return future generations to sanity, self-awareness, and spirituality.

# CHAPTER 7: PARENTING IN A RACIST SOCIETY

"We are not likely to find the answers to the problems of African American people by asking the same people who put the hole in the ozone, who let atomic energy get out of control (Three Mile Island and Chernobyl), who can't control the stock market, who can't stop polluting the earth, and who don't seem to be able to teach our children, even the basic things like reading and counting. We must learn to trust our own wisdom again." – Asa Hilliard III

"For too long the task of defining and understanding the reality of Black family life has been relinquished to non-Black scholars. Because of their cultural blindness, in many instances, these researchers have given incorrect interpretations and *explanations of Black reality.*" – *Nobles and Goddard (1984)*

We are at war. African American children are at risk, and they must be redirected. The future of our children and their children are at stake.

Over the course of writing this book I had many enlightening encounters with parents. One day, I was standing in line at a deli counter when I spotted an African American sister with a new baby. In my best Dr. Huxtable imitation I said, "That's a fine baaaby. Boy or girl?" The proud mother said with a broad grin, "Girl, and she is three months old."

I introduced myself as a professor of early childhood education at Clark Atlanta University. She asked if I knew Barbara, and naturally I did. (Professor Barbara Mason was the coordinator of the middle grades education program.) The new mother identified herself as a middle grades teacher. I asked if she had family in the area, a mother or mother-in-law? Both lived far away, so my new friend was pretty much on her own.

I asked, "If you were to purchase a book on parenting or parent education, what would you want the book to say?" She said, "What do I do during the first eight weeks?" Her response was consistent with many new mothers who do not have family support nearby.

African American parents face so many challenges raising their children. In addition to managing family relationships or raising children on their own, they must continually fight a hostile, uncaring society for themselves and their children. No other group of people in America has ever been confronted with the racism that African American parents deal with overtly or covertly.

We hear a lot about the progress we have made as a people, but the reality is, the struggles we face in raising African American children in the 21st century are not very different from those our parents faced during the past century. Civil rights leaders, activists, and other advocates for social justice continue unfolding the many atrocities of racism that seemingly will not go away.

Arming African American children against racism is our mandate as parents. We have the arduous task of raising resilient children who must feel good about themselves and who can function in a racist society—even while America looks down on them, patronizes them, and the most evil of all, conspires against them. Parents must show them how to keep their eyes on the prize and not let racism deter them from dreaming and having visions of greatness. I'll never forget the story Malcolm X told in his autobiography about wanting to be a lawyer and his

live. If the generations growing up today do nothing more than indulge in self-gratification and ignore the needs of the African American community, we will be doomed. However, if these generations grasp the urgency of our plight, and armed with knowledge and understanding of our history and culture take action against racism, they will help usher us into a proud, productive future.

> "The lasting challenge that we face is the absence of information and understanding of African culture. This has been by design. The enforcers of an oppressive system work to create cultural disorder among the oppressed. In particular, they suppress the value of other cultures while glorifying and fabricating the history of themselves. They understand that the resulting disorder will make it impossible for the oppressed to be truly independent." (Hilliard, *African Power,* 2002)

### The Kwanzaa Mandate

Kwanzaa is a celebration that occurs during the last six days of the American calendar year and the first day of the New Year. Kwanzaa joins together the cultural elements of Africans on the continent and around the world. Dr. Karenga, the father of Kwanzaa and the seven principles (*nguzo saba*), tells us that the cultural values and practices represent the different continental Africans from all parts of the Motherland and is truly a spirit of Pan-Africanism.

This may be a leap of faith or optimism, but if African Americans would embrace the *nguzo saba* and practice them, not only during Kwanzaa but year round, then our positive future survival would be assured. The following are the seven principles. I encourage all African American parents to incorporate these classic community-building ideals into their daily parenting.

- Unity (*umoja*): to strive and maintain unity in the family, community, nation, and race.
- Self-determination (*kujichagulia*): to define ourselves, create for ourselves, and speak for ourselves, instead of being defined, named, created by, and spoken for others.
- Collective work and responsibility (*ujima*): to build and maintain our community together and to make our sisters' and brothers' problems *our* problems and to solve them together.
- Cooperative economics (*ujamaa*): to build and maintain our own stores, shops, and other businesses and to profit from them together.
- Purpose (*nia*): to make as our collective vocation the building and developing of our community in order to restore our people to their traditional greatness.
- Creativity (*kuumba*): to do always as much as we can, in the way we can in order to leave our community more beautiful and beneficial than when we inherited it.
- Faith (*imani*): to believe with all our hearts in our people, our parents, our teachers, our leaders, and the righteousness and victory of our struggle.
  (Madhubuti, 1987)

If parents will use the *nguzo saba* as a blueprint for academic and cultural excellence, their investment in time and effort will nearly guarantee success for their children. Creatively applying the seven principles during the various childhood development stages will be the saving grace of future generations.

# CHAPTER 8: WHERE DO WE GO FROM HERE?

"You're either part of the solution or part of the problem." – (Leroy) Eldridge Cleaver **(1935–1998)**

In 1968 the late Dr. Martin Luther King, Jr. published his book, *Where Do We Go from Here?* In it he asked, "Where are we?" and "Where do we want to go?"

Current events suggest we are facing urgent challenges nationally and around the world. We must arm African American children academically and culturally to deal with the challenges that they will undoubtedly face in the future—the repercussions of unwise decisions made by governments, institutions, and corporations today.

From grassroots activism to political and corporate governance, African Americans are fighting on many fronts. Still, it is easy for ordinary parents to feel overwhelmed by the magnitude of the problems facing our community and families. What can one parent, one family do?

Beyond the advice given in this book, which focuses on best practices in childrearing, I strongly encourage all African American parents to reach beyond their homes and become involved in the community and greater society. This is the way excellent full potential parents become outstanding African men and women.

First step: become active in your child's school. Let's be honest. Too many African American parents have given into the distractions of life and have neglected becoming involved in the very institution that is charged with the holy task of educating their child! This is insanity!

There is no excuse for not becoming involved in your child's school. If you work and/or stay at home, give time every week to helping teachers in the classroom. Working parents must find a way. Attend after-work and weekend PTA meetings or local community meetings that convene to discuss school issues. Schools understand that parents work and can't always take off, and many now organize meetings and events with this in mind. Also, talk to your employer about wanting to become more involved in your child's school. Many companies have enlightened policies about volunteerism, and this would certainly include mentoring students at your child's school, supporting teachers in the classroom, going on field trips, etc.

Over the years I've noticed a growing hostility between parents and teachers. Even in the most cordial of interactions, the negative feelings simmer beneath the surface. When I was growing up, the teacher's word was law among students and parents. Parents completely trusted teachers to do their job, and teachers respected the all-important role of the parent. If there was a discipline problem in the classroom, the teacher was allowed to take care of it, for better or worse, often with a ruler to the back of the hand. African American teachers often lived in the same neighborhood with their students. This created strong parent-teacher relationships.

Today, teachers complain that parents don't support them in the areas of discipline and homework. They say that many parents won't even come to school to pick up their children's report cards. They tell me horror stories about parents threatening violence against them, often in front of students.

# Where Do We Go From Here?

Parents have their horror stories, too. About teachers refusing to give time and attention to their children. Bright children being ignored because class discipline problems demand the teacher's time and attention. In one recent example, two eighth graders took it upon themselves to request a transfer out of a particular classroom because the teacher had lost control and they weren't learning anything.

Both parents and teachers have valid points. We must begin to form true partnerships by honestly discussing the problems and resolving them. The future of our children is at stake. And as the example of the two eighth graders demonstrates, our children *want* to learn.

Parents want safe schools and safe walking routes for their children. Fathers, here is where your help is desperately needed. If you are available during the day, volunteer to provide security in the school building, outside on school grounds, or along walking routes to and from school. Too many of our children are getting to school late because they must go the long way to avoid gang territory. Metal detectors in some schools create an unhealthy, prison like atmosphere that interferes with the learning process. Fear inhibits learning. Safety facilitates learning.

You may feel inclined to get involved on a governance level. In Chicago, for example, local school councils (LSCs) provide community-based oversight for school administration. Parents and community residents run for office and serve designated terms. Even if there is no such body in your community, surely there is a PTA (Parent Teacher Association). You must attend these meetings! PTAs provide useful functions, including fundraising, sponsorship of school spirit events, and more. Along with other parents, fight for higher academic standards and nutritious cafeteria meals. Help raise money to bring into your school foreign language instruction, the arts, sports programs, and physical education. Make sure that after school programs do more than just babysitting. Bring in a program that will support the academic goals of the school with tutoring and mentoring programs. Problems can be solved. You have to be persistent and demanding. Your direct interest and participation can make the difference.

*We Are Family*

One innovative idea involves reaching beyond the nuclear family into the extended family. In the September 2005 issue of *Ebony*, comedian George Wallace said that his family wanted the younger children to understand the high expectations that have been laid upon them in terms of their school work and future careers. At a very special family reunion, children met relatives who were scientists, educators, university officials, lawyers, professional athletes, and corporate professionals. The goal was to let children know that academic achievement was within their reach. They too can accomplish what other family members had achieved. Your family may or may not have such a lineup of successful individuals, but they are somewhere in your environment. Seek them out and let your children know that they too can reach high levels of success.

My daughter writes the last chapter in From Roots to Wings. After over hearing Jamille and her mother talking about motherhood, I asked her to write what it has meant being a parent. This chapter, therefore, is for expected Moms. It is her journey entries for expected moms with high hopes for their expected child. Dr. Fu-Kiau talks about the importance of preparing the next generation. We hope that we did our best in getting her ready for the joys of parenting.

# Chapter 9: The Joys of Parenting: The Next Generation
## By Jamille E. Bradfield

Anticipation. Excitement. Anxiety. Nervousness. These are the feelings that consumed me as I headed to Walgreens to pick up a home pregnancy test. It was Sunday, May 19, 2002, a day I will never forget. A day that changed my life in the most perfect way imaginable. Of course, that's second to the day that I married the most wonderful man in the universe.

Like most women, I know my body. I knew something was different. The idea of being pregnant and becoming a mother raced through my mind.

My loving husband, William, and I had been happily married for more than three years. We had been trying to and conceive a child, but the initial attempts were unsuccessful. We listened to advice, both solicited and unsolicited, from family members and friends. After taking it all in and trying to follow at least some of the suggestions, we decided it was too stressful. Just when we came to the conclusion that if it was meant to be it would happen…it happened!

On that Sunday afternoon in May, I told William I thought I might be pregnant and was going to take a pregnancy test. When I returned from the drug store, I went to the bathroom, closed the door, opened the test, and read the instructions carefully. I took my time, as I didn't want to make any mistakes. Silent and nervous, I watched as one pink line appeared in the result window and then another line appeared. It was official, at least by home pregnancy test standards, which are 99 percent accurate. I was pregnant!

I hurried into the family room to tell William. He smiled in his usual laid-back way and then began asking questions. We were leaving for a vacation and a friend's wedding in Napa, California, in just five days and he wanted to know if it would be safe for me to fly. Great! It was our first trip to wine country, and now I wouldn't be able to enjoy a single glass of wine. But believe me when I say that I could have cared less about wine or anything else for that matter. It was all about my baby now.

After having my pregnancy confirmed and getting the thumbs up to travel from the doctor's office the next day, William and I decided we would go ahead and tell immediate family and our closest friends. We would wait to tell other people after I had made it through the first trimester. Of course, that didn't last very long. We were too excited to withhold the news and ended up telling everyone within the first 12 weeks.

William and I, both natives of Atlanta, Georgia, have lived in Dallas, Texas, since we married in 1999. Our families still reside in Atlanta. We called my parents first. To say they were elated would be an understatement to the nth degree. This would be their first grandchild. They congratulated us, and we continued with our first round of calls.

Over the years, my wonderful mother-in-law would often say things to me about having a baby. She would refer to a baby as having a little "pitty pat." It was common knowledge that this was her catch phrase, so when we called her and my father-in-law to tell them, William and I silently counted to three and then began chanting in unison, "Pitty pat, pitty pat." They broke out laughing, as they knew exactly what we were telling them without actually saying it. They too were excited. This would be their fourth grandchild.

# The Joys of Parenting: The Next Generation
## By Jamille E. Bradfield

Next, we called grandmothers, siblings, and best friends to share the news. Everyone was genuinely happy for us.

Later that week, we left for Napa, California, to attend my friend's wedding. Since neither of us had ever been to Northern California, we decided to extend our stay and visit San Francisco for a few days. Unfortunately, we weren't able to fully enjoy the sights because Mr. Morning Sickness decided to tag along. Nevertheless, we had a great time, and what a wonderful way to celebrate the news that we were going to be parents.

The week after we returned from vacation, I had my first prenatal appointment. My OB/GYN examined me and took an ultrasound. I was six weeks pregnant. He told me my due date was January 28, 2003, a date that would later change a few times. He gave me a copy of the ultrasound photo, which just melted my heart, even though the black and white image of the fetus resembled a cashew. Then he discussed basic prenatal care and allowed me to ask questions.

I was on my way to holding the most honorable title a woman can have—mother.

Over the next few months, I bought all sorts of books and magazines on pregnancy, baby names, and designing baby nurseries. I loaded up on fruits, vegetables, and yogurt because I wanted to eat healthy for the baby and myself. Of course, that was before my cravings of grape soda and cheeseburgers set in.

I was equally excited and scared. Like most mothers-to-be, I worried about something going wrong. I approached each pregnancy milestone, such as the next trimester or tests for genetic disorders, with a heap of anxiety. I'm sure watching countless episodes of traumatic births on the Discovery Channel's popular show *Labor & Delivery* did not help.

# FROM ROOTS TO WINGS:
## Successful Parenting African American Style

My first real nail-biting experience was waiting for the results of the genetic disorders tests. You see, William is adopted and does not know anything about his biological father's medical history. When I was filling out paperwork on our parents' medical backgrounds, I honestly had no answers to questions about his paternal lineage and had limited information on his biological mother.

To my surprise, I was not nervous at all about actually having my blood drawn for the tests, as many adults are. I simply turned my head until it was over. It was the week or so of waiting for the results to come back that kept me on edge. As a matter of fact, even though I knew a week had not passed, I began calling the doctor's office to inquire if my results were back yet, just in case they had come back earlier than usual. No such luck.

I kept asking myself, "What if this or that is wrong with my baby?" How would we handle it? How would we cope if the baby was born with a genetic disorder, lived for a few months or years and then died? What if…?

However, when the doctor's office finally called, my bundle of nervous energy proved to be all for naught. All tests came back negative. Needless to say, it was a tremendous sigh of relief for us both as we cleared the first hurdle on our way to having a healthy baby.

One other scary moment during my pregnancy was when we discovered that I had uterine fibroids. I did not know at the time that this condition is common among African American women. Because of the location of the fibroids, my doctor opted early on to do a C-section. Now a lot of women in today's society would be emotional and upset by this sort of news, but I was completely

# The Joys of Parenting: The Next Generation
## By Jamille E. Bradfield

fine with it as I had witnessed one of my best friends, Trion, give natural birth to my goddaughter Tori several years earlier. As beautiful and miraculous as it was (my girl is a genuine trooper), I knew that I did not ever want to go through the pain of labor if I could avoid it even a little bit. Plus, that whole explanation by comedienne, Carol Burnett, that likened childbirth to pulling your bottom lip up over your head did not exactly paint the prettiest picture of my inevitable big day. In my mind, I went through a quick checklist. Let's see…pre-scheduled C-section, thereby foregoing the pain of contractions, an epidural, anesthesia from the neck down, plus my baby would not be born with a head shaped like Yoda's. I said, "Where do I sign up?"

Of course, as months progressed and people learned that I would not be doing the whole natural childbirth thing, I was accused of being a chicken and taking the easy way out. My response to all was a nice and simple, "WHATEVER!"

The doctors (I had to visit all of them in the office so they would be familiar with me and my pregnancy in case one of them was on call when the baby came) monitored the fibroids' growth throughout the pregnancy. Fortunately, the baby continued to thrive and obviously reigned supreme in terms of getting the ample blood supply it needed to grow. In fact, we discovered later that the fibroids had essentially died due to a lack of blood supply. As it has always been, here was yet another reason to fall down on bended knee and thank God.

As the months went by, I started the dialogue with William about baby names and nursery décor. He of course wanted us to take our time and wait until the last trimester. Last trimester? Had he gone completely insane? Was he having a sudden, temporary lapse of memory? Had he forgotten that he married a woman who is a natural-born event planner? I told him to stop being silly and get serious as we had some life-changing decisions to make.

Now, what you have to understand about William is that while he is basically a cool, calm, and collected person, I knew that deep down inside he was just as excited as I was, as was evident by the little things he often did to surprise me. For instance, once when I expected the baby's nursery furniture to arrive a week or two later, William, who told me he had a doctor's appointment that afternoon, actually came home for lunch early and met the delivery guys. He put the crib, dresser, and hutch together and had all of it set up when I came home from work. Until then he had just painted the room. I walked in there daily daydreaming of what would soon be a full-fledged baby nursery.

We talked about needing to purchase a new, family-sized sedan to accommodate our new addition (not to mention the fact that my growing belly was nearly touching the steering wheel on my little Honda) but never really went out and test-drove anything. One day William told me he needed me to drive him to a Nissan dealership across town. He had already started the paperwork on a new car in the exact color I wanted and with everything I wanted in it.

And we're not going to even talk about how many pictures he took of me. Well, maybe just a little. I cannot resist. We had a designated backdrop in our house (okay it was a blank wall in the formal dining room) where every month we took an official "belly" photo to chronicle my expanding waistline. He purchased a new camera and video camera in preparation for the big day as well as all of the precious Kodak moments to capture after our little bundle of joy arrived.

# The Joys of Parenting: The Next Generation
## By Jamille E. Bradfield

As months continued to fly by, we found out in my fifth month that we were going to have a...GIRL! I was surprised (only because without any substantiation, I had convinced myself it was a boy) and simultaneously excited. William's initial reaction was different. Even though he still denies it, his facial expression said it all. I believe he too had convinced himself it was a boy; plus I knew he really wanted to give his father a grandson. Learning that we would be tasked with raising an African American girl in America in the new millennium was a surreal experience. A new set of worries started to set in, but not for long as we were too excited about sharing the news and meeting her.

William bought me a device called the Womb Song, and I used it to read and sing to the baby. I had read articles that described ways to bring an intelligent baby into the world, and even though many of these activities were not proven, I refused to be outdone by any other mothers-to-be out there in the world. I was striving for academic excellence for (notice I didn't say from) my child long before she ever took her first breath outside of the womb.

I played Mozart, Bach, and Beethoven through this device that I strapped to my belly almost every night during my second trimester (until it became uncomfortable). When the strap became too short to wrap around my stomach, I just held it in place. And when I wasn't playing classical music, which has been said to stimulate the brain, I sang. And when I wasn't singing, I read *The Three Musketeers* by Alexandre Dumas or Daniel Defoe's *Robinson Crusoe* and sometimes even articles from the *Dallas Morning News*. The roots of academic and cultural excellence were being planted.

Fast forward. Believe me when I say that I reviewed all 10,001 names and their origins in my baby names book. We decided on the name Kennedy Noelle, not for any particular reason other than we really liked the name.

We were blessed with five baby showers (two in my hometown of Atlanta and three in Dallas) which yielded enough baby gear to open our own Babies R Us store! We decorated the baby nursery with a Baby Ballerina theme in pink and lavender.

We asked my friend Trion and our other dear friends, Kim and Dwayne Wright, to be Kennedy's godparents.

We interviewed and visited a handful of daycare providers. You often hear parents-to-be say they visited numerous daycare centers. I did not start off with a humongous list of daycare centers for one simple reason. I knew the type of person and environment I was looking for. Period.

I grew up in a house of educators. Perhaps I should be more specific. Make that early childhood educators. And since you've reached the final chapter of my father's book, you probably know by now a little bit about what he does and the knowledge and expertise he has gained and shared over the years in the area of helping to shape the minds of children and helping their parents and teachers understand what it takes to realize a child's full academic potential.

As I prepared for our first daycare site visit, I called Dad and asked him about NAEYC (National Association for the Education of Young Children) accreditation and what it meant. After he broke it down to me, including the part about him participating in the writing of the guidelines for the NAEYC accreditation standards (why was I surprised), we focused on facilities that had

# The Joys of Parenting: The Next Generation
## By Jamille E. Bradfield

the accreditation. Few did and those that did were either too far, too expensive, or in my opinion, too crowded for a three-month infant to start, which is how old the baby would be when I returned to work.

With all of the horrific things you hear in the news today about abuse towards babies and young children in daycare centers, we were extremely particular about who we were going to trust with our precious daughter. We were also concerned about all the airborne germs and diseases floating around. We did not want our daughter staying at a facility with an infant room crowded with infants and toddlers, a high staff turnover rate, or untrained staff who may not adhere to policies and procedures of cleanliness and hygiene.

In the end we decided on Ms. Eunece "Nece" Snow, a small, licensed, in-home childcare provider who had been recommended to us by friends and who would later turn out to be God sent.

Last but not least, with a C-section scheduled for January 22, 2003, we decided to spend our last childless Christmas together quietly. We did not spend an unreasonable amount of money on gifts. After all, we already had the best gift of all who was kicking me regularly by then. No traditional holiday dinner with more food than we could possibly imagine or eat. Just a couple of steaks on the grill and the two of us together with our feet up (not that I could see mine), watching football.

We were all set. The nursery was complete. My hospital bag and baby's bag were packed and ready to go. Our family's and friends' telephone phone numbers had been written. My mother was scheduled to fly in a couple of days prior to the C-section.

# FROM ROOTS TO WINGS:
## Successful Parenting African American Style

*Arrival*

On Thursday, January 9, 2003, I went for my routine weekly prenatal checkup. All was well but I told the doctor, Dr. Wesley Brady, that I felt more pressure than usual and wanted her to check and see if the baby had dropped. She did with caution and said, "No, she's still pretty high. Everything's fine. We'll see you next week."

I returned to work at Greyhound's corporate office, responded to a few e-mails and voicemails, and then drove to a nearby Steak 'N Shake (one my favorite burger places) for a to-go lunch. I went back to the office and sat down to eat when I started having abdominal cramps. The uncomfortable feeling continued until I stood up to stretch and then...my water broke! I could not believe this was happening to me. This was not how I had it all planned out.

Indulge me for a moment as I share words that actually came from my lips on the drive over to the hospital (my co-worker Karen who was also expecting her first baby, drove me). Me, the ultimate planner, said things like, "I didn't have a chance to get my eyebrows arched and my pedicure." "My mother is not here yet." "I skipped the chapters in my pregnancy books on labor!" "I'm not supposed to be feeling any pain." "This was not a part of my plan!"

In the midst of all the excitement, I quickly remembered that I was not in control. This was God's plan, so I needed to just sit back, relax as much as was humanly possible, and get ready to enter the wonderful world of motherhood just about two and a half weeks early. So I checked into Presbyterian Hospital of Dallas,

# The Joys of Parenting: The Next Generation
## By Jamille E. Bradfield

got settled in the pre-operation room, and graciously received my epidural (right in the middle of a contraction).

Shortly after William arrived at the hospital, the nurses got him suited up and they wheeled me into the OR for the C-section surgery. Everything happened so fast. Our daughter was born at 3:14 p.m. CST on January 9, 2003, weighing in at 6 lbs., 11 oz. The rest, as they say, was history, but in this case it was *her*story.

She was the most perfect little person. My mother arrived on the last flight from Atlanta to Dallas later that same day and of course, she was beside herself to see her baby with a baby! I'm certain it took her back to when my brother and I were born. My in-laws, Gladys and Cephus Bradfield, were equally as excited and couldn't wait to see their new grandchild.

William and I spent the next three days in the hospital getting to know Kennedy and how to take care of her. Then, Monday rolled around and it was time to take Kennedy to her new home and begin a new chapter in our marriage and in our lives—as parents.

*Awareness and Appreciation*

Over the first couple of months, we experienced all of the usual suspects that come with taking care of a newborn: sleep deprivation, every-hour-on-the-hour diaper changes, the ever-so-gentle baths, the feedings, the pumping of breast milk at 2:00 a.m. while watching reruns of *Love Boat* and *Cheers* on Nick at Nite while William gave Kennedy a bottle. It was a routine unlike anything else we had ever done before.

It was during this time that we became acutely aware of how much dedication, attention, and teamwork it took and would continue to take to raise a baby from infancy. Expressions of verbal appreciation for mothers and fathers around the world who had already been through what we were experiencing were repeated in conversations between us rookie parents.

And if I haven't already said it, William is a REMARKABLE father. He goes way above and beyond what many fathers are willing to do when it comes to helping out at home with all of the baby's needs, all while making sure Mommy is happy and comfortable. A good friend of fellow parent, Hubert, told William early in my pregnancy four simple words that he sort of adopted as his unofficial motto around the house: *Happy Mommy, Happy Baby.*

Shortly, after we returned from our first trip to Atlanta with Kennedy at the tender age of eight weeks, we began to change the routine at home just slightly to prepare her for a new schedule. Baths were now being followed by a warm bottle while being rocked in the glider and listening to classical music (trying to keep that little brain stimulated). Bedtime of 8:00 p.m. was initiated and enforced ever since Kennedy turned three months old because we felt it is important for Mommy and Daddy to have some quality, uninterrupted adult time every evening.

At this point I had roughly three more weeks of maternity leave before I was to return to work. I was getting nervous about turning her care over to someone else and guilty about not staying home to care for her full-time.

In the meantime, we took delight in her every whim. She was a beautiful, healthy baby girl and was on track, actually a little ahead of herself, on her developmental milestones.

# The Joys of Parenting: The Next Generation
## By Jamille E. Bradfield

We always talked to her just like we talked to each other. We never used the traditional ga-ga, goo-goo language that can turn adults into goofy, oversized Disney characters, and we always made a concerted effort to pronounce words properly and speak correct English. No Ebonics and no curse words in her presence.

Some of our people might read this and accuse of us of trying to raise our child as if we were White. To that I would respond, "Since when does a strong command of the King's English and a yearning for knowledge make someone White?" That is the level of excellence we should be striving for. The bottom line is that we want to expose Kennedy to as much academia and cultural arts as we can to broaden her scope on what life has to offer, understanding that she will have to compete with the best to secure her piece of pie in the world one day.

We have tried to give Kennedy a nice, solid start in life. We want the best that our money can buy for our little princess, especially when it comes to her education, because we know how important a good education is and how it can impact your life.

We started a college savings for her. We made conscious decisions to buy some stock for her first Christmas instead of spending an outrageous amount of money on toys, even though we did buy a few.

I began doing some preliminary research on daycare programs with an educational curriculum. Nece only keeps children until a certain age. She stressed to us early on that she was not an educator and that she encourages all parents to eventually move their children to a center where they will receive the educational foundation that is ultimately necessary for their academic development.

Once again, my list wasn't very long because I knew that I wanted Kennedy to attend a Montessori school and found one that sounded like the perfect program. The North Garland Montessori School (NGMS) looked like an official international Montessori school and boasted an impressive curriculum.

I printed out some information from the school's Web site and shared what I had learned with William. Although he wanted to wait until after Kennedy's first birthday had passed to even begin thinking about where she would go next, I told him that the best schools had waiting lists and that if we wanted our daughter to attend the best school, we needed to start applying right away.

As the months continued to zoom by (boy, people aren't kidding when they say time goes by quickly), Kennedy amazed us day after day. At six months, an important mid-point milestone toward her first birthday, we were truly enjoying her. No more sleep deprivation because she was sleeping through the night. No more pumping milk as she was completely on formula, and the diaper changes were a little farther apart than before.

We starting using the Baby Einstein brand of flashcards and showing her the Baby Nursery and Baby Mozart video series.

Yes, we were gliding on easy street, enjoying our daughter. We were even beginning to talk about having another child in about two years. We had this parenting thing down. Then, as Emeril Lagasse would say when he's adding something special to one of his signature Cajun dishes, "BAM!" Just when we thought we could not have been blessed anymore than with the wonderful little family God had given us, we learned that I was pregnant again! Kennedy was only six months old, and she was going to have a baby brother or sister. Our children would be a mere 14 months apart in age.

# The Joys of Parenting: The Next Generation
## By Jamille E. Bradfield

Peggy, one of the nurses in my doctor's office, still jokes with me about the day I came in to have an official pregnancy test. "Are you absolutely sure?" I asked in disbelief, to which she replied, "Yep, you're pregnant!"

I cannot even share William's initial reaction to the news. Although it was hilarious (we still laugh about it), it is not fit for print. We were both in a sort of mesmerized state at first. Then as we recovered from the initial shock, we quickly snapped out of it and became excited all over again. That is, until we had flashbacks of middle-of-the-night feedings, diaper changes, mixing formula, etc. That would be our reality again in about eight months.

So now we would have not one, but two children to love, raise, dream for, and of course worry about. I started my baby planning frenzy all over again, albeit not quite as intense this time around since I generally knew what to expect.

I was just as anxious to learn the baby's gender as William, and I had decided that our second child would be where the buck stopped as far as our contributions to repopulating the world. Thus, this would also be the last biological opportunity to give my in-laws a grandson—the only chance of having that coveted male heir who could carry on the Bradfield name.

As always, God was on our side. During my second trimester we were thrilled to learn that this time we were going to have a healthy little boy. I will probably never know how proud William was to deliver that news to his father, Cephus Bradfield, or "Big Daddy" as the grandkids affectionately call him.

By this time, Kennedy was 10½ months old. She was crawling, pulling herself up, and saying her first words. She was a quick study, always mimicking what she saw or heard and always extremely alert and inquisitive. Of course, the closer we got to her first birthday, the more I began to revisit North Garland Montessori School as a topic of discussion.

We celebrated our first Christmas with Kennedy that year along with my parents and brother, Jimmy, at our home in Dallas. A few weeks later we had a huge first birthday party at the house for Kennedy, something we would later conclude was a little excessive and more for us than for Kennedy who did not really understand the gist of what was happening. Nevertheless, we had a great time sharing her special day with some of our closest friends (and a rather memorable clown/magician), and that is all that really mattered.

In my last trimester, William completed our son's nursery and got everything ready for the big day. Again, I was scheduled for a C-section—same doctor, same hospital. This time things went smoothly and according to plan. No surprises.

On March 25, 2004, our son Chase Alexander was born, weighing in at seven pounds, four ounces. God had blessed us tremendously with beautiful, healthy children.

Today, with Kennedy at 2½ years old and Chase at 1½ years old, our conversations about the future center around our children's education. Kennedy, who is now in her second year at North Garland Montessori School, is excelling and has a vocabulary of a five-year-old (and no I'm not exaggerating, it is true). Chase will join his big sister at NGMS in a couple of months. God willing, they will continue Montessori school at least up until kindergarten. Then we plan to move to one of the better public school districts here in the Dallas/Fort Worth metroplex.

# The Joys of Parenting: The Next Generation
## By Jamille E. Bradfield

Of course, being the planner that I am, I have already done research and proposed to William the community we need to move into and which public schools (elementary through senior high) they should attend based on the school's most recent accountability ratings (exemplary being the highest in the state of Texas). In looking at these schools I am also considering factors like diversity in student population and extra curricular activities. Being well-rounded and exposed to different cultures is just as important to me as test scores in math and science.

Speaking of cultural excellence, another thing that attracted us to NGMS, which is a member of the International Montessori Council, was the different cultures represented. The makeup of both the student and teacher population is extremely diverse in terms of ethnicity. There are African Americans, White Americans, Europeans, Asians, Latinos, Indians, and the list goes on. The principal and executive director of the school believe in exposing children to the native languages and cultures of their teachers. For example, Kennedy's (and soon to be Chase's) teacher in the toddler class is from Germany and teaches German to the older classes.

As a sidebar, all of my schooling (from preschool through college) was in African American-only institutions. I know my parents made the best decisions for me and my brother as it relates to our education during that time, but today, more than three decades later, we live in a world where co-existing and working with people from other races and backgrounds is crucial to survival and competitiveness, especially in the business world. We want our children to be around children from other backgrounds early in life.

Back to North Garland Montessori...the school DEMANDS the utmost respect and manners from its students beginning with the 18-month-olds. As NGMS parents, we had to make a commitment to refrain from allowing our children to view any and all TV programs or music that are violent, sexually explicit, or mature in theme. The solution was simple. We resolved that the children could only watch *PBS Kids, Noggin,* Disney programs, or an educational DVD, such as *Dora the Explorer, Barney, Blues Clues,* etc.

The school also has a small student-teacher ratio that allows for more one-on-one interaction. The students learn through a hands-on approach. Instead of just learning about science and nature through textbooks, they maintain a garden and petting zoo on the campus. Parents are involved with the school and all of its activities.

Last year, students in the elementary class kept journals and turned them into little books. Nine students participated in the project and the books were sold to parents at $18 each, netting each participant $2 per book sold. They learned at an early age how to become authors and get paid for their writing.

Overall, I believe we have chosen the right path for our children in terms of establishing a strong path to achieving academic and cultural excellence. Other things that will come into play in the next few years are the extracurricular activities they become involved in. We want to give them piano, golf, and/or tennis lessons. We want Kennedy to take ballet, both to play soccer (which is big in Dallas), martial arts, swimming—so many things we want to expose them to.

# The Joys of Parenting: The Next Generation
## By Jamille E. Bradfield

The key is to get them started in a couple of activities and as they get older let them decide what they like or have a gift for. We will not, under any circumstances, become "Sideline Dad" and "Stage-Mom-from-Hell," forcing them into doing what we want or trying to relive our dreams through our children as so many parents do.

We will simply raise our children to finish what they start and to always give their all and do their BEST in whatever they set out to do in life. Mediocrity is unacceptable.

On a final note, I know that we do not and will not have all the answers. We're finding our way as parents every single day. But we both have generations of values and traditions to draw from. William and I were given roots with the strength of Samson, and as a result of those roots and the continued guidance and support of our parents, we developed wings as young adults that have allowed us to soar to new heights in our marriage, professional endeavors, and in life.

In the constant pursuit of excellence as parents, I leave you with this poem that was given to us by Nece, the children's first daycare provider. A copy of this poem lives on our refrigerator door.

**Children Learn What They Live**
**by Dorothy Law Nolte, Ph.D.**

If children live with criticism, they learn to condemn.

If children live with hostility, they learn to fight.

If children live with fear, they learn to be apprehensive.

If children live with pity, they learn to feel sorry for themselves.

If children live with ridicule, they learn to feel shy.

If children live with jealousy, they learn to feel envy.

If children live with shame, they learn to feel guilty.

If children live with encouragement, they learn confidence.

If children live with tolerance, they learn patience.

If children live with praise, they learn appreciation.

If children live with acceptance, they learn to love.

If children live with approval, they learn to like themselves.

If children live with recognition, they learn it is good to have a goal.

If children live with sharing, they learn generosity.

If children live with honesty, they learn truthfulness.

If children live with fairness, they learn justice.

If children live with kindness and consideration, they learn respect.

If children live with security, they learn to have faith in themselves and in those about them.

**If children live with friendliness, they learn the world is a nice place in which to live.**

# Reflections

Parents, a quality education is a must if African American children are to survive and thrive as the 21$^{st}$ century continues to unfold. Students of the 21$^{st}$ century are expected to know more than previous generations. WE have a responsibility to the next generation. An education that embraces academic and cultural excellence benefits the individual student, the family and the immediate community. Remember instill the idea of determination, patience and courage into your children. You must also be patient and supportive. If not our children's natural genius will never be released, simply because we did not pay attention to their development. We need not debate what shape they are in, especially, our males. Each of you has at least one major decision to make as it relates to your children. The question remains – what are you prepared to do?

# Appendix A

## Supplementary Information to Enhance Development and Learning: Attitude

Children must be mentally prepared to thrive in the environment where knowledge is the new capital. The millennium in which most of their lives will be lived out requires knowledge, skills, performance in the use of technology, resourcefulness, ability to use and apply information sets, the ability to make decisions, work with or supervise people that do not necessarily look like them, and the ability to change and adjust to new situations.

African American children are born with natural genius. Hopefully, reading *From Roots to Wings* will empower you to take the reins, if you have not, of shaping your children's future in becoming academically and culturally astute. Education continues to be the avenue that offers the best path to improve the African American lot in the American society, if not in the new global economy.

Children are natural learners. They learn at their own rate and in a variety of ways. They learn by doing, playing, exploring/discovering, initiating, and through trial and error. The following information provides some insight relative to each of the content areas that children will encounter at home or in school. In an earlier chapter, Dr. Asa Hilliard reported how attitude impacts on learning. Your child's attitude towards learning can either impede or enhance what is to be learned.

# Appendix A

Attitudes about learning begin at home. Children should have age appropriate tasks or responsibilities to do. You help children develop a positive attitude by the way you teach them to complete a task. The manner and tone of talking to them can impact on how they approach the things they have to complete. By fulfilling these tasks, children begin to develop self-confidence and independence. Similar attitudes apply to learning. You can help by motivating them to successful completion of duties and responsibilities. Children should be responsible for starting and completing tasks. If they are challenged with something that appears to be difficult, you can assist, but do not do it for them. You can demonstrate the number of steps involved in doing the task. Positive attitudes are necessary for success as a student and as an adult in later life. The points listed below are applicable at any time during the lives of young learners.

Teach them and encourage the development of positive attitudes by demonstrating that you as a parent have healthy attitudes toward learning yourself. Learning different things provides opportunities that challenge their abilities and leads to success, and provides feedback about their capabilities. It further provides situations where they can ask questions and get answers for their efforts. Remember family habits, customs, and traditions start when your children are exposed to the kinds of experiences that are worthy of being carried forth to the next generation.

## *Development and Learning: Problem Solving*

In this world of high stakes testing, it is important to teach our children how to solve problems. When it comes to word problems, many African American children are challenged. Therefore, it is important to provide as many opportunities as possible to strengthen this area. Problem solving is the thinking process children go through from the time that a problem appears until it is solved. There are several steps they must remember and systematically follow:

1. Define the problem.
2. What are possible solutions?
3. What information is provided and what additional information is needed?
4. What solution do I choose and try?

Remember, figure out what is wrong and proceed from that point. The family and home environment offer many opportunities to solve problems. Children should also know that there are problems even moms and dads cannot solve either.

### *Development and Learning: Reading*

Ninety percent of what children learn requires them to be excellent readers. Excellent readers have healthy attitudes about books and other reading materials. Children learn to read when they have reading role models. Parents who read generally transfer that attitude and behavior to their children. All children should have a library of books. Children should visit neighborhood libraries often. Parents should read to young children every chance they get. An attorney friend who has three daughters said she read to them through high school. Together they read passages from selected books. She helped them to carry out critical analyses and

# Appendix A

inferences from what was read. The daughters graduated from undergraduate college with honors. One received an MBA, one became a chemical engineer, and the other a CPA. Remember, children must first learn to read and then read to learn.

## *Development and Learning: Math*

Always let African American children know that math had its beginning in Africa. All one has to do is to look at the pyramids and ask, "How did they know how many blocks were needed? How did they know how high to make it or how much space to give it? How long did it take to build?" Pyramid building utilized highly advanced mathematical concepts of computation, measurement, space, and time. In addition to doing addition, subtraction, multiplication, and division, children should be given chances to apply their problem solving skills to solve math problems.

## *Development and Learning: Science*

The process of science is something that all of us are involved in on a daily basis. Science goes far beyond someone walking around a laboratory in a white coat. Science is a way of thinking and doing. Science is a way of finding answers by asking questions. It is information about the world and people who live in it. What you eat and when you eat has to do with science. When you go into the elements, you must wear clothing according to weather conditions. That is science, too. Science is everywhere, every day. Initial attitudes and skills relative to science are learned in the home. When children are taught to wash their hands after playing, before eating, or following use of the bathroom, they are learning and utilizing scientific principles. Much of what is learned about weather, water, air, land, rocks, plants, and people is scientific information. Information from these sources is generally used to make decisions and solve problems. The scientific process is the same for first graders as it is for graduate students doing post-doctoral work. The process involves the following steps:

1.  Purpose: decide what it is you want to learn.
2.  Research: find out as much as possible about the topic.
3.  Hypothesis: predict the answer to the problem.
4.  Experiment: design a test to confirm or disprove the hypothesis.
5.  Analysis: record what happened during the experiment.
6.  Conclusion: was the hypothesis correct?

Experiments can be very simple. For example, what happens (Purpose) when you apply heat to an ice cube? That is the idea to be tested. We know (Research) that when water is frozen, it is at or below a certain temperature. When that temperature changes (above 32 percent), the ice will melt (Hypothesis). An ice cube can be placed in a glass so that it can be watched (Experiment). The temperature in the room is 72 degrees, therefore, the ice cube will melt. After a period of watching, the ice cube melts (Analysis). It is determined that ice cubes will melt (Conclusion) when placed in water above 32 degrees in temperature. This simple experiment demonstrates how easy it is to apply the scientific method. It is important for children to learn these steps. By doing so, they will develop excellent critical thinking skills. Science is creative thinking.

# Appendix A

## *The Early Learning Kit*

The Early Learning Kit is made up of items found in homes or at school. The kit was designed to allow young learners and parents or other adults to interact. If possible, when children are allowed to use the kit, it should be done with a parent or adult some of the time. The time should be of high quality. Quality time helps to shape attitudes and modify behaviors. Quality interactions provide the basis for motivation and stimulation to learn.

Items were selected for the purpose of improving children's language development, thinking skills, mathematic concepts, ideas related to exploring and discoveries in science, large and small muscle development, and eye-hand coordination. When parents and children talk about the items in the kit, social development is being nurtured. Skills needed for academic success in school can be learned when items in the kit are used appropriately.

Children learn best when they are provided with opportunities to explore and to discover on their own. The role of the parent should be to facilitate these various activities. For example, if a child is working on assembling a pattern of blocks but runs into some difficulty, the parent should assist by asking questions relative to being stuck at that point. A parent should not immediately make the correction, unless the child appears to be frustrated or wants to give up. Here is yet another opportunity to encourage children to not give up easily when problem solving. When all is said and done, you may ask, "Did I do enough?"

The Child P.L.A.Y (Parent Learning Activities for the Young) Kit was developed for use with parents in the Family Initiative project. The staff presented each mother with a kit to help them help their children (0-3) to understand the importance of early literacy. The kit included but was not limited to the following items:

- My School Box
- Drawing paper
- Jumbo pencils
- Small chalk board
- Crayons
- Assorted color modeling clay
- Chalk of various colors
- Modeling clay board
- Clay hammers
- Cookie cutter
- Lacing shapes
- Large lacing beads/board with tying strings/zippers
- Easy grip pegs
- Letter blocks
- Jump rope
- Duplo blocks
- Scissors
- Finger paint
- Magic markers
- Games, books, ethnic pictures
- Masking tape
- Primary paper and newsprint
- Number and alphabet cards
- Praise songs
- Puzzles (simple to complex)
- Word games

# Appendix A

The above list contains basic items. You can add to it as your child gets older.

*Prospective Parent(s)*

When planning for or expecting a child, prospective parents should have a library of books on babies. This is a must list of reading materials for parents-to-be. These suggested books are not to be used in lieu of information from your health care provider or medical doctor but as resource materials in your preparation to becoming parents. No book can answer the infinite number of questions you have. Nor can any set of reading materials relieve you of all of your concerns and apprehensions. However, this short list can help to answer *some* questions and allay *some* fears.

1.  Marshall, Connie, (2000) R.N. *From Here to Maternity*. The presentation of information in this book is based on standards for Obstetrics-Gynecologic Services and Guidelines for Perinatal Care. The American College of Obstetricians & Gynecologists (ACOG) and the American Association for Pediatricians (AAP) 2000-revised edition, Conmer Publishing, N.V, publish it.

2.  Murkoff, Heidi, (2002) Eisenberg, Arlene, And Hathaway, Sandee, B.S.N. *What To Expect When You're Expecting*. This book provides information essential to the health and welfare of mothers prior to, during, and after pregnancy. It prepares parents for the important job of nurturing those young lives. *What To Expect When Expecting* is probably one of the best sources for the non-medical persons of up-to-date, detailed, medically sound advice in print. More than ten

million copies have been sold. Revised 2002, Workman Publishing, NY.

3. Hogg, Tracy, (2001) *Secrets of the Baby Whisperer*. Information and advice from this book gives parents the ability to develop early insights into their baby's temperament, a framework for interpreting a baby's early communication and behavior. It also offers practical and workable solutions to correct typical infant problems, i.e., excessive crying, frequent feedings, and sleepless nights. Ballentine Books, NY.

4. *The Good Housekeeping Illustrated Book of Pregnancy & Baby Care*. The book contains more than 800 color photographs. This book provides photos on pregnancy and birth, baby care, and health care. Published 1999 by Hearst Books, NY.

5. Hale, Janice E., (2001) *Learning While Black* provides information on how Blacks can learn despite the racial treatment Blacks, especially males, continue to receive. She gives a personal account of what she experienced as a single mother who made a conscious effort to give her son the best possible education. Published by The John Hopkins University Press, Baltimore.

6. Talbott, Emma M., (1997) *The Joy and Challenge of Raising African American Children*. Her book provides information on one who has tried through trial-and-error practical ways of successfully raising African American children. Her presentation is a firsthand account of raising two sons. Published by Black Belt Press, Montgomery, AL.

7. *The African American Holiday of Kwanzaa*, The University of Sankore Press. A classic in the growing body of books on

# Appendix A

Kwanzaa, this work is a must for parents who are committed to providing a rich cultural experience for their children.

Also, consider purchasing instructional materials that are sanctioned by organizations that are nationally acclaimed. The following publishing companies often write or develop their books along the lines of national standards:

- American Education Publishing Company
- American Heritage High School Dictionary
- Hayes School Publishing Company
- Instructional Fairs Publishers
- McGraw-Hill Publishing Company
- Milliken Publishing Company
- National Geographical Map Series
- Scholastic Materials
- Steck-Vaughn Publishers

An investment in a computer and developmentally appropriate instructional games, CDs, and videos, along with proper interaction with your children, will do wonders to improve and enhance your student's learning.

# Appendix B

**The High Scope Educational Foundation List of Characteristics**

The following is the complete list of characteristics we used to collect information from the education majors in the Full Potential survey. Only those items with ratings or tallies of at least 35 or better were included.

Circle the 10 characteristics listed below that you consider most important for your children to succeed at school. Draw a line through those characteristics that you would not want to encourage.

| | | |
|---|---|---|
| Affectionate | Is a good guesser | Adventurous |
| Altruistic | Asks questions | Competent in basic skills |
| Careful | Competitive | Conforming |
| Considerate | Cooperative | Courageous |
| Courteous | Creative | Critical |
| Desires to excel | Determined | Domineering |
| Emotional | Energetic | Faultfinding |
| Fearful | Friendly | Healthy |
| Gets good grades | Industrious | Independent |
| Intelligent | Intuitive | Negative |
| Obedient | Persistent | Physically strong |
| Proud | Quiet | Rebellious |
| Refined | Receptive | Remembers well |
| Self-confident | Self-satisfied | Self-sufficient |
| Has a sense of humor | Sensitive | Sincere |

Socially well-adjusted    Stubborn          Talkative

Timid                     Thorough          Versatile

Is a visionary            Is a risk taker

# Appendix C

## We Must Never Turn Our Backs on Our Children, Never!

In today's world, parents have to be fierce, protective, and tenacious in the process of rearing children. "Back in the day" things were quite different. Parents basically left their children in the hands of their mothers or grandmothers or "big mommas." Favorite aunties were also used to help in the rearing when others were not available. Unfortunately, the idea of the village as we knew it has changed. As a result, we have, unconsciously, neglected our children. Further, we have disconnected from the great history of our ancestors. We must establish rituals that are as sacred to us as the Bar mitzvah is to the Hebrews.

### *A Subject Matter Checklist for Parents*

How well are you helping your child(ren) in their work in and beyond school? Here is a sample checklist to see how you are doing. Make this a daily habit or as often as you can. Use this tool to enhance your child's development and learning, both in and out of the classroom.

Put a check before each true statement.

\_\_\_\_\_ 1.  I read something every day. My child sees me read often.

\_\_\_\_\_ 2.  I have a variety of reading materials at home.

\_\_\_\_\_ 3.  I read to my child at least four times a week.

\_\_\_\_\_ 4.  I have a library card.

\_\_\_\_\_ 5.  I take my child to the public library at least two-three times per month.

_____ 6. I encourage my child to write notes, letters and lists of things.

_____ 7. I listen while my child shares the day's activities.

_____ 8. I take my child on brief excursions (even to the store) and expose him/her to things that will build communication skills—speaking, reading, writing, and listening.

_____ 9. I play word and listening games to help develop the above skills.

_____ 10. I play games with numbers.

_____ 11. I help build skills in place value (ones, tens, hundreds, thousands, etc.).

_____ 12. I help my children count in multiples (5, 10, 15 or 3, 6, 9, or 11, 22, and 33).

_____ 13. I let my children read prices in the store, newspaper, and catalogs.

_____ 14. I help my children learn fractions by cutting or slicing things to see parts of the whole. I compare sizes to show differences. I measure things to show amounts.

_____ 15. There is a scale in our house.

_____ 16. There is a dictionary in our house.

_____ 17. There are family games in our house.

_____ 18. There are times we eat as a family and talk about daily events.

_____ 19. There are duties and chores assigned to my child.

_____ 20. There are limits to the number of hours my child watches TV.

Post this checklist in a visible place (like the refrigerator) to remind you of the many ways you can easily create a learning environment in your home.

# REFERENCES

*Acknowledgements*

Burnett, Zaron. 1992. Keynote Address: "Attributes and Characteristics of Excellence," Top Ladies of Distinction, awards
banquet, Trenton, NJ.

*Introduction*

Hilliard III, Asa. 2002. *African Power*, Gainesville, FL: Makare
Publishing Company.
Kunjufu, Jawanza. 2002. *Black Students, Middle Class Teachers*.
Chicago: African American Images.
Nobles, Wade. April, 2003. Keynote Address: Nsaka SunSum
Conference. Atlanta: Clark Atlanta University.

*Chapter 1: The Full Potential Movement*

Donovan, Suzanne M. & Cross, Christopher, T., Eds. 2002.
"Minority Students in Special and Gifted Education,"
National Research Council Report. Washington, DC:
National Academy Press, 2002, p. 51.
Kearney, K. & LeBlanc, J. May/June 1993. "Forgotten pio-
neers in the study of gifted African Americans,"
*Roeper Review*, Vol. 15, No. 4. The Roeper School. pp.
192–199.

### Chapter 2: The Ideal Child

Hilliard III, Asa. 2000. "Twelve Challenges and Twelve Powers of African People," unpublished paper.

### Chapter 3: Gifted and Talented Parenting

Berreuta-Clement, Schweinhart, & Weikart, 1984. Changed Lives: The Effect of the Perry Preschool Program on Youth Through 19. High/Scope Educational Research Foundation. Ypsilanti, MI.

Fu-Kiau, K. Kia Bunseki & Lukondo-Wamba, A.M. 2000. *Kindezi: The Kongo Art of Babysitting*. MD: Black Classic Press.

Fu-Kiau, K. & Bunseki, Kia. 1988. *The Kongo Art of Baby Sitting*. New York: Vantage Press, p. 1.

Hill, Robert. 1972. *The Strengths of Black Families*. New York: Emerson Hall Publishers.

Hilliard III, Asa. 2002. *African Power*, p. 8.

Sigel, I.E., McGillicuddy-DeLisi, A.V., & Goodman, J.J. 1992. *Parental Belief Systems: The Psychological Consequences for Children* (2nd Ed.). Hillsdale, NJ: Lawrence Erlbaum Associates, Publishers.

Wilson, Amos N. 1991. *Awakening the Natural Genius of Black Children*. New York: Afrikan World InfoSystems.

### Chapter 4: Parents as Teachers

ABC News & *20/20*. Sept. 30, 2005. "Fantasia's memoirs reveal experiences with illiteracy, rape." http://abcnews.go.com/ 2020/print?id=1170655.

# References

Cantave, Cassandra & Harrison, Roderick. Nov. 2000. "Historical Trends II: The Educational Progress of African Americans." Washington, DC: Joint Center for Political and Economic Studies.

DuBois, W.E.B. 1961. *The Souls of Black Folk*. Fawcett Publications, Greenwich, CT.

Hombo, Catherine & Mazzeo, John. (2000). "NAEP 1999 Trends in Academic Progress: Three Decades of Student Performances, NCES 2000-469 U.S.," Department of Education. National Center for Education Statistics. Washington DC: Education Publications Center.

Kunjufu. *Black Students, Middle Class Teachers*.

National Alliance of Black School Educators. 1984. Saving the African American Child (Report). Washington, DC.

Willie, C.A. Reddick, R.J. 2003. A New Look at Black Families (5th ed) ALTAMIRA Press Rowman & Littlefield Publishers, New York.

Woodson, Carter G. 1969. *The Mis-education of the Negro*. Washington, DC: The Associated Publishers, Inc.

## Chapter 5: The Role of Fathers

Billingsley, A. 1968. *Black Families in White America*. Englewood, NJ: Prentice-Hall, Inc.

Comer, J.P. & Poussaint, A.F. 1992. *Raising Black Children*. New York: A Plume Book.

Santrock, J.W. 2001. Child Development (9th ed). McGraw Hill, Boston.

Young, J.C. & Hamilton, M. 1978. "Paternal Behavior: Implications for Parenting" In Mother Child Father Child Relations. Washington, DC: NAEYC Publications.

## Chapter 6: Ancestral Connections to Excellence

Hilliard, Asa III. 1995. *The Maroon Within Us*. Maryland: Black Classic Press.

## Chapter 7: Parenting in a Racist Society

Anderson, Margaret. 1958. *Children of the South*. Delta Publishing Company.

Baldwin, James. 1985. *Evidence of Things Not Seen. Random House, New York*

Comer, James. 1989. Young Children, Volume 45, NAEYC, Washington, D.C.

Hilliard III, Asa. *African Power*.

Kitwana, B. 2002. *The Hip Hop Generation*. Basic Civitas Books. NY

Karenga, M. 1988. *The African American Holiday of KWANZAA*. Los Angeles, CA: University of Sankore Press.

Madhubuti, Haki. 1987. *Kwanzaa: A Progressive and Uplifting African-American Holiday*. Chicago: Third World Press, pp. 5–6.

Nobles & Goddard. 1984. Understanding The Black. A Black Family Institute Publication Oakland, CA

Wilson, Amos N. *Awakening the Natural Genius of Black Children*.

## Chapter 8: Where Do We Go from Here?

King, M.L., Jr. 1968. *Where Do We Go From Here?: Chaos or Community*. Boston, MA: Beacon Press.